PIETRO MARILLI

SEARCH MARKETING
DESIGN

Where to find your next customer and when

Foreword by

Alberto Mattiello

Contributions by:

Maurizio Bramezza
Fabio Chisari
Gabriele Di Matteo
Gaetano Grizzanti
David Herzog
Alessandra Modenese Kauffmann
Anna Ponticiello

Marketing is not the art of finding clever ways to dispose of what you make. In short, marketing's job is to convert people's changing needs into profitable opportunities. Marketing's aim is to create value by offering superior solutions, saving buyer search and transaction time and effort, and delivering to the whole society a higher standard of living.
(Philip Kotler, Marketing from A to Z)

INDEX

"MAY YOU LIVE IN INTERESTING TIMES"

Alberto Mattiello
Head of Future Thinking Project at J. Walter Thompson

"Do you need a new marketing book?"
When Pietro Marilli shared with me his SEARCH MARKETING DESIGN, his question seemed worth reflecting. To contextualize my answer, I started from a warlike metaphor: marketing today is an environment that for companies can remember the arrival of American soldiers in Iraq in the first Gulf War.
At the time they defined an unprecedented and unexpected war environment with an acronym: V.U.C.A..
V means *Volatile*: things could change very quickly, unpredictably and often for the worst.
U stands for *Uncertain*: there was no possibility of planning because the information was often incomplete, not well defined and above all did not allow us to imagine with certainty the results.
C is the initial of *Complex*: the environment was not easy to understand as it required different disciplines, and it was not enough to remain at knowledge's surface to be able to govern practices.
Finally, *A* as *Ambiguous*: often things were open to different interpretations, removing certainties in every phase of strategic planning.

It is clear to me that the evolution of marketing over recent years has great similarity with V.U.C.A. In fact, marketing is learning to adapt in a world of continuous transformation: a world where artificial intelligence has learned to contest fines, write songs and recognize the mood of consumers; where the 5G shifts the horizons of sharing platforms to previously unimaginable levels; where quantum processing reveals a near future with infinite computational capacity. A world where, in the coming years, everything can, and is going to happen.

It is therefore easy to recognize the volatility of social platforms and marketing techniques: one day they seem to be destined to the monopoly of a certain type of relationships and in a few months, they may risk extinction. If you think about it, in the past a small modification of the algorithm of Google or Facebook has been enough to eliminate entire types of agencies and consultancy models. The uncertainty of the result is a factor with which we have learned to make peace and the complexity of the technology we must handle has reached a point where it becomes virtually impossible to have full awareness of it.

If you are not a computer engineer or a quantum physicist, try the thrill whenever you try to explain how Blockchain technology or a Quantum Computer works. And the ambiguity of the phenomena we face every day is therefore an effect that perpetually compels us to always give new interpretations to the planned events.

After all, marketing has become a discipline that is based on a cycle of continuous transformation. Typically to a Change phase, one of Change Management is followed by a Stability phase. Now one change follows another unabated and the management of change has become a perennial state.

And for this reason, now more than ever, we need interpretative models and a lot of passion for the newer.

As we read in SEARCH MARKETING DESIGN, in the age of data it is the questions that determine the success of our actions. To understand the context and plan a marketing strategy in a V.U.C.A. it is crucial to ask the right questions and above all to ask continuously if the reference frameworks are still valid.

It is therefore not a question of knowledge, rather an approach to knowledge.

In fact, it is not enough to add new information or models, it is often necessary to have the courage to abandon these certainties that are no longer adequate to the new context.

The thing that is good for is to put everything in a historical perspective, starting from the roots of marketing and the evolution of digital search to produce a future vision.

Do you still need a new marketing book? In the current context, what is needed is not to describe what is happening but to inspire what is possible. And we do not just need continuous reflections and updated models.

From marketing, which has been active in the VUCA world for at least 15 years, we expect a much more strategic role: in companies it is up to marketing people to drag organizations into this new digital culture. Starting from who leads organizations.

An ancient Chinese saying said: "may you live in interesting times".

As marketers it is undoubted that we are, but this sentence can be a blessing and at the same time a warning.

SEARCH MARKETING DESIGN is a guide to this fierce change and here you can find the keys for turning interesting times into opportunities.

WAS ANOTHER BOOK ON WEB MARKETING REALLY NECESSARY?

The question is legitimate. I have asked it myself several times, I have reflected several months. If I finally came to this answer - this book – it was for a necessity, which became the objective and the driving force of my writing: to try to explain digital marketing in a simple and concrete way, from the perspective of a businessman.

Generally, most manuals are written by trainers: I am not a trainer nor have anything against those who do it, but I think that sometimes it is more useful to deal with those who work for years, experiment, head in small and large real life cases.

My ultimate goal is to exchange views, that is explaining, evaluating, reasoning, stimulating, maybe even intriguing, to learn how to avoid the big mistakes that cost companies missed opportunities, time and lots of money.

But this does not mean delivering ready-made, dogmatic knowledge: this book does not contain - *it cannot contain* - in any way - the secret recipe for an easy and successful web marketing. Indeed, I think that a universal rulebook should not exist, and that we must always treat each situation, every business and every market as a different story.

"Do not trust, my boy, of those who promise to make you rich from morning to night. Usually they are crazy, or they are cheaters"– C. Collodi

---

This book, rather than pretend to give definitive answers, tries to help you to think about contexts, people, needs, questions.

Questions; people have been asking questions on-line for years; I was asked the same questions by my clients, as abruptly as effectively, by large, but also very small businesses, even by artisans. Mostly, my clients had a decidedly relaxed but active attitude towards the digital world. They listened to what I had to say, the promises of the online world, tried to understand their dynamics but then they always went straight to the point: what would I gain? How do I sell? How much does it cost me and how much I sell? How much do I get, in short? They had no interest in knowing how, with which website, to what effect and in what colours. But they were interested in knowing what the return on the investment would be.

However I find that not everyone shares this sensible approach anymore, especially the larger companies, and often I hear them say "You cannot ask how much you'll earn ..." as if they must have total and undisputed confidence in a consultant, an agency, a philosophy as that is a sensible thing to do.

Web marketing, as well as marketing in general, also has these responsibilities: listening to concrete needs, thinking about congruent strategies, letting oneself be judged based on data, numbers and results.

I believe that my first interlocutors were the most precious people in my professional growth. With their frankness, their directness and colourful ways, even their ignorance (I mean regarding the digital world) they urged me to ask the right questions and try to get the right answers.

Many years later this *best practice* "to ask oneself" remains a driving principle, to which we always return and hopefully never waver.

Enjoy the book!

Pietro Marilli

MODERN ENTREPRENEUR'S HEADACHE

There was a time when people wondered what the Internet was like: "Do you have it?", "Did you try it?", "Do you use it?". That time has clearly passed a long time ago. According to the annual Global Digital Survey, in 2018 internet users worldwide exceeded four billion (53% of the world's population), an increase of 7% over the previous year. Of these users (mostly connected by mobile), over 3 billion are also active on social networks: YouTube and Facebook primarily, following WhatsApp, Facebook Messenger and Instagram.

The pervasiveness of the connection, the use of social networks, the omnipresence of smartphones has changed the way we see and stay in the world. For sure, it has changed the way of buying and selling; the market, the concept of enterprise.

For some, it has created more possibilities, time savings, an increase not only in turnover but also in profitability. But on the other side of the coin, it has come at a cost: more competition, more options and tools to use, a company - and a customer idea - in a fast changing environment to keep up with.

And that's how entrepreneurs, including myself, live a continuous digital headache.

Once, before the web was born, it was relatively easy: it was about making a good product or having a good product to sell. The most fortunate or rich could spend a large amount on advertising, especially on TV, and the feedback was (almost) assured. Today this system does not work anymore, things have changed.

But the digital revolution is not only given by the Internet, Google or Facebook. It is the whole that makes the total. It is the fact that technology has allowed unprecedented logistics, that people have started using a smartphone over 150 times a day to connect to the network and learn, that Amazon has become the number one competitor, that even a small shop in the city cannot be sure of not being at stake.

Ok, we are all in play, but what are the rules of this game?

There are a lot of opportunities, but where can I find them?

There are a lot of tools available, but which ones are best for me?

There are a lot of agencies and professionals, but who to trust?

Here's how the headache of the modern entrepreneur is born.

Think digitally, think differently.

For some managers, it's about technology. For others, digital is a new way to interact with customers. And for others, it's a completely new way of doing business. It is tempting to look for simple definitions, but to be meaningful and sustainable, digital must be seen less as a thing and more as a way of doing things. [1]

This reflection is useful for introducing our speech. It is no longer a matter of choosing whether to have a physical store or an e-commerce, to campaign on Facebook or Google, to have a website or lots of landing pages to send traffic to. It is no longer about how-to bring traffic. It is not just about trying to be online, to stand in front of people who could, or should (if we talk about old-fashioned targets) be interested in your products. It is something completely different. Indeed, it's not a "thing", but an approach.

The Search Marketing Design, beyond any technical definition, is exactly this. Approaching

---

[1] "What 'digital' really means" by Karel Dörner e David Edelman – McKinsey, July 2015

*digital more strategically than tactical. Listen
before speaking. Think before doing.*

It means understanding goals and exploring opportunities before embarking on adventures that may be expensive and not profitable at all.

It is a matter of stopping for a moment and then being able to go fast and smoothly. A moment of "delay" is useful as you tie your shoes before starting a marathon.

In concrete terms, it's about knowing that you do not need to be anywhere, talk anywhere, spend money to be visible everywhere. Because "everywhere", "the world", "all", you do not need them at all.

"Every day about 3.5 billion searches are done on Google, but probably 99.9% of these people do not need it. What allows you to stand out is to meet and convince the 0.1% of people ready to buy, that are the right people"

The purpose of this book and of Search Marketing Design is exactly this: to define a new model for completely new times and dynamics.

There are three components that interact on this strategic approach:

1. *Search*: has the objective of recalling the qualified traffic on digital search engines (organic or paid) because it is the only one that allows to intercept those who are clearly expressing a need (they are looking for something) and therefore are (potentially) ready to buy. It is therefore the ideal kingdom in which to intercept the question. Facebook on the other hand, as well as

other social or other forms of online visibility (native advertising / display, etc.), is instead the ideal place to launch messages that could be captured, raise and awaken a latent desire or need.

2. *Marketing*: because marketing comes first of web marketing.
3. *Design*: not only because we must adapt each message to the customer's most satisfying experience, but also because, in a way, we need to trace, design and tailor-made strategies for their behaviour.

BEFORE STARTING, MORE CLARIFICATIONS

Before starting, more clarifications seem to me necessary and useful for readers.

This book is designed for those involved in business: entrepreneurs, CEOs, business managers, marketing directors. For this reason, the book often flies over information technology that ultimately would make the text complex and not very understandable. The idea is to disclose a message and not explain exactly every single mechanism.

The book's structure follows a principle of "awareness": knowing the dynamics in order to make better decisions. But the parts have been designed in such a way as to leave the reader wide freedom to move in the text according to their needs.

In the first part we will analyse the online research process, as prepared by the engines and as experienced by users, focusing on the concept of *relevance* as the fundamental objective of a company's online presence.

In the second part we will retrace the classic concepts of marketing considering the digital revolution.

In the third part we will define the most suitable strategies to draw a plan of success.

FIRST PART: SEARCH

WHEN WE HAD THE YELLOW PAGES

"The web is not limited to connecting machines, connects people" – Tim Berners-Lee

---

Until a few years ago if you needed a plumber because you had flooded the bathroom or the washing machine had a leak, if you were looking for a house painter who would give a nice refresh at home, if the TV had dropped dead just during Sanremo's week and urgently needed a visit by an electrical engineer, the solution was always the same: the mammoth yellow book that was delivered together with the telephone subscription. Since 1967 the Yellow Pages have been the search engine of the Italians, who could find answers to their needs and questions with relative comfort sitting on the sofa at home.

Today this instrument has fallen into disuse, almost forgotten: an archaeological find of our recent past now buried in some dusty corner of our homes because it has lost some or all its meaning, its usefulness. The same applies to similar objects, such as the Tuttocittà or road atlas, or even the Encyclopaedias. But also, paper and pen on the table next to the phone. Or the calendar next to the fridge.

Today knowledge, information can be read on a screen. The effects of this transition not only in society but also in our brain are the subject of discussions and investigations. "Google makes us stupid", someone said provocatively (but not much).[2] Someone else has proved that makes us lazy, because we tend to no longer remember information but only the place where we have them available. In practice, we have made our devices connected to our brain's hard drive.[3]

Since the Internet has taken hold in our lives, since the material published online has become increasingly widespread, covering almost every sector of human knowledge, the traditional channels dedicated for searching for information - paper, for the most part - have been supplanted from web pages, to which the search engines, the interface of any online consultation, lead with surprising efficiency.

As everyone knows, a search engine is an automatic system that, based on one or more keywords, analyses a set of data from its database and returns an index of available contents, positioning them according to an algorithm.
Without search engines, the web would be like an oil field before the invention of the auger. Or like the bag where my wife never finds the house keys.
Billions of web pages crammed into servers all over the planet; all the human knowledge in it would be useless if they were not reachable (and easily). Today it seems obvious, but in the early years of the web it was not like that: it was played blindly.
When a query was made - "interrogation" - on the first pioneering search engines (Excite, InfoSeek, Lycos, Yahoo! and AltaVista), it

---

[2] I refer to the famous speech by Nicholas Carr on Atlantic, which gave wide impetus and renewed the debate on the topic:
 https://www.theatlantic.com/magazine/archive/2008/07/is-google-making-us-stupid/306868/.
This article then turned into a book, also translated into Italian. The author claims that the Web is reprogramming our brain in its image and likeness: accustomed to frantically passing through different sources, we are becoming superficial and we are sacrificing our ability to be focused and think critically and in depth.
[3] Betsy Sparrow et alii, *Google effects on memory*. Article published in *Science*: http://science.sciencemag.org/content/333/6043/776.full

was like throwing a line, hoping that it would bite something, even knowing that nothing would be coming out.

The ability to give relevant results to user queries and expectations was what differentiated and selected the first protagonists of this sector of the network, bringing out the dominance of Google, born in 1998. No one else, not even Msn Search, created by Microsoft and integrated natively into the Windows operating system, managed to tarnish its dominance.

"What Larry Page and Sergei Brin had in mind was a goal so candidly insane as it was simply philanthropic: making all knowledge of the world accessible: accessible to anyone, easily, quickly and free. The great thing is that they have succeeded" – Alessandro Baricco

---

FROM PERTINENCE TO RELEVANCE

In 1998, typing on Lycos the word "car" jumped out a screen full of porn sites.[4]
Why? Lycos' algorithm, like the first versions of the same Google, was limited to analysing the frequency of a given word (a keyword), thus choosing whether it was relevant with the search for users.
Porn sites owners, like other categories, were supported by an army of black hat SEO professionals [5] and began to exploit the system to

---

[4] Tim Harford, *50 things that have made the modern economy*.
[5] n SEO terminology (search engine optimization), black hat SEO refers to the use of

promote their products in the ether. It was simply to insert the word "car" on the pages to jump to the top of the results.

Sometimes the word "car" was hidden in the folds of the code or written "white on white" and invisible to users. However, *spiders* who were searching the web were stupid enough to fall for it

It did not take a short time to move on to a more evolved system, but inexorably we got there.

> *"After all, this is an economic exchange: Google transforms reputation into attention (in traffic); sites turn attention into cash" – C. Anderson*

Today the algorithm of Google, secret and in some ways indecipherable, works on a multitude of factors such as CTR[6], the time spent by users on webpage, the social confirmation signals, the links that refer to the determined one page and the authority of the sites linking it; plus, a slew of technical factors and human supervision. Indexing has become more precise, complete and relevant: in short, more useful and satisfying.

Companies want to see themselves placed on the front page, but the complexity of the algorithm now definitely discourages the do-it-yourself and makes it appropriate to rely on SEO specialists (i.e.

---

aggressive strategies, techniques and tactics that focus only on search engines and not on a human audience and usually do not obey motor guidelines of research. Some examples of black hat SEO techniques include keyword filling, invisible text, doorway pages, adding keywords that are not related to page content, etc. (from webopedia)

[6] Click-through rate (initialled in CTR) ("Percentage of clicks" in Italian) is a rate that measures the effectiveness of an online advertising campaign. If a banner or advertisement displayed on the World Wide Web is displayed 100 times (impression delivered, every time a banner is uploaded to a web page and it is displayed on a user's screen) and a person clicks on it, the CTR will be 1%; it is therefore considered a significant indicator of the user's interest in the proposed message. (Wikipedia)

professionals who can jump out the site in the right way when a user throws his keywords line).

The real turning point that allowed Google to dominate the world traffic, however, took place with the definition of a new parameter, linked no more to the algorithms but to users: relevance was added to the pertinence. It marked the transition from meeting search engine criteria to meeting user expectations. A small Copernican revolution.

"I have more fun and have more financial success when I stop trying to get what I want, and I start helping others get what they want" – S. Johnson e L. Wilson

---

To allow it was the introduction by Google' Search Intent, or the continuous attempt to really understand what the user is looking for, where and why. Let's try to understand it better.

THE SEARCH INTENT

To define a user's search intent, even the simple introduction of "Maybe you were looking for this?" when a query is not perfectly understandable it was a big step forward that allowed Google to double its traffic: if I am distracted and I type "assurances", the search engine includes my error and suggests the correct "insurance". Today, the development of search voice commands (Ok, Google?), linked to the surge in traffic from mobile, further facilitates the user in navigation: speaking is faster than writing (150 against 20 words per minute), I can do it simultaneously with a thousand other things, and the spelling becomes another problem![7] It is therefore estimated that by 2020 voice and image-based searches will involve 50% of users.

If we just type in "insurances" in the search engine, however, Google does not know what (why) we're looking for. Do we want an insurance package? An additional pension? Do you do a research on the insurance institution? Know how much they pay for an injury?
The autocompletion module tries to guess the intent based on what "other people have asked": it suggests, for example, to be more precise and specify if I look for insurance "online, travel, car, motorbike, home, life, mandatory for lawyers".

Even the first results provided on the webpage try to clarify what my expectations are. And basically "related research" comes.
At the same time, the research has evolved in a semantic sense: Google no longer looks only at the keywords of the queries, but also their implicit aspect, using the data provided by the device and the context. For example, if with an iPhone geolocated in Milan (implicit element) I make a query "plumber 24 / 24h" (explicit element), the two things add up and Google will tend to give a mobile-friendly website as a better result to inform me about where to find a prompt plumber intervention in Milan.

Search engines are therefore constantly busy understanding the query and the user's expectations, to provide a relevant result.
As far as I know, *relevance* never had the honour of being the word of the year (as opposed to *fake news*), but it should have. *Relevance* - the correspondence with the user's research intention - is the figure of our world and of our market. It should be the first rule and the first thing to keep in mind to do business. In digital it becomes an

---

[7] Observation: before putting on the market a product with an unpronounceable name ... it is better to ask a department store for the unsold.

absolute imperative: either you are relevant, or you are out. That's all.

For an entrepreneur or a company that wants to be online, understanding the search intent of their users, their cause, their expectations, allows for example to create content and landing pages that best meet their needs. Knowing why a user is searching for something helps to build content to answer questions as clearly as possible, perhaps even covering queries and topics that are immediately relevant and related, without users having to go back to a search engine (and therefore point to other companies) for more information on the same topic.

If those who offer a product or service, therefore, perhaps even extraordinary, cannot be proposed by the search engine when it might interest someone (i.e. be relevant to him) ... for the web is invisible. If then, once seen, you do not offer the answers to the user and in the best way ... you are discarded.

You must not just be there. Visibility must be targeted.

You can imagine Google as a judge (we fly over the concept of partial / impartial) that evaluates the responses of a process: weighing the pertinence and relevance of the content in relation to the question (to search) of users.

Greater vigilance and accuracy in evaluations determine greater satisfaction for users, but also greater competitiveness among producers and managers of content (including advertising).

Seeing your own recipe for pasta amatriciana at the top of the results was quite simple in the early 2000s, but it is very complicated, almost impossible, in 2018.

The same happens with any product and service you want to promote. Cars, real estate, professional services, spare parts, dinners and guided tours, life tips are all competing. On average, in Italian language only, it is easy to find yourself competing with at least one million results. We gain the user's ability to have relevant answers, but it becomes clearly more difficult to emerge in the competition and meet the user who is looking for something we have to offer.

"Google loves you only when everyone else loves you first." - Wendy Piersall

---

A WORK WEEKEND IN GOOGLE

With so many people looking on the Mountain View engine research and trusting for purchases and services, with such competitiveness, the next step by Google was the introduction of a system to ensure a preferential place in the results: "first on Google" to be clear.

In October 2000, AdWords and pay per click were born, the online advertising services with which Google found its commercial meaning (to date these services are the main source of revenue for the colossus).

The system is very simple: a company creates its own ads and the search engine places them on its pages, positioning up to four above the results not paid. The ads are selected and made visible through the umpteenth algorithm that, among the many variables, considers the keywords searched by the user. In doing so, ads are not placed anywhere indiscriminately, but are relevant to the user's and company's goals.

You do not place a sign on a busy street, hoping that someone wants to buy a new car. It is about promoting your dealership when someone is looking for a new car and paying only when a user clicks on the ad and comes to hear what you have to offer.

Until May 2002, however, AdWords did not do its job very well. Eric Schmidt, executive director of Google for ten years, relates:

"On a Friday afternoon in May 2002, Larry Page (the founder and CEO of Google, ed) was playing around with the Google site, entering search terms and verifying the results on advertising he got. He was not happy with what he was seeing. He entered an expression for the search, and while Google returned a rich and organic set of relevant results, some advertisements were completely unrelated. A search like "Kawasaki H1B" returned a lot of advertisements by lawyers who aided immigrants to obtain an H-1B visa, but none related to the vintage motorcycle that was the subject of the search. Or the search for "paintings in the French caverns" returned a plethora of advertisements from online retailers who obviously had no assortment of paintings in the French caves (or even facsimiles). Larry was scandalized by the fact that the AdWords algorithm, which decides which ad works best with a certain search string, sometimes proposes such meaningless messages. [...] He printed the pages containing the results he did not like, he highlighted the incriminated advertisements and posted them on a bulletin board in the canteen, next to the billiard table, with a large letter written in title: THESE ADVERTISEMENTS ARE DISGUSTING. Then he went home."[8]

What Eric says happened later is even more interesting. A group of engineers recognized the mistake and (during the weekend!) started working to solve the problem. At 5 am on Monday, he was presented via e-mail with the solution, a new implementation of the engine. It was based on the calculation of a new index, which would have since rewarded the results with a precise, new and revolutionary criterion: "from that moment the advertisements should have been placed according to their relevance and not to what the advertisers would have been willing to pay".

---

[8] Schmidt, Eric. *How Google work.*

PSYCHOLOGY OF RESEARCH

In 2017 the Iab Forum in Milan invited me to talk about SEO, Search and how to win customers for a business. When I shared the theme of my speech, *"Psychology of search"*, the moderator did not object to my topic, but I could see that he was taken aback. He was very kind and nice, as all of the staff at Iab, in a mixed state of confusion and curiosity, gave me a brief and open introduction, trying to understand where I wanted to ward off, I thank him for giving me the opportunity to share what I do and love.

On the other hand, just a few days before the event, I had a very different conversation with a journalist from the Corriere della Sera. He called me to talk about entrepreneurship and digital, about the relationship between Google and the money that comes in or rather does not come into the coffers of entrepreneurs and shopkeepers. Then too, I said: "Let's talk first about research psychology". My interlocutor was surprised and did not hide the embarrassment: "No, I'm sorry we'd like to talk about how to be found on Google".

Exactly. We speak precisely of this.

Why Google makes over $95 billion in revenues? Why did advertising spending in digital channels exceed the traditional ones in 2017?

The reason is very simple: because research works. And I'm not saying that SEO or Search work, I'm talking about something else: I'm talking about the fact that it works for people.

Let's take an example. Think of a person you like to confide in, talk to in difficult times, ask for advice. Why him/her?

You could say because you love her, because you know her well, because you trust her. Sure, but the most important reason is probably that she understands you. Being understood has always been the most powerful lever. Google makes money, it is the best search engine, it is synonymous with the web, because it understands people and every day takes a further step forward in this direction.

Companies that are on top of searches, which get more clicks and presumably have more revenues, are successful for the same reason: they understand people.

That's why we talk about research psychology. It is not that at night we have all become shrinks. We simply understood that what we call "research" are expectations: The Search to be effective must respond with importance to the needs of users.

But how do you become relevant? Where do you start?

HOW TO CALM DOWN A BABY THAT IS CRYING?

Imagine being in a room with a crying baby. He starts to cry slowly and then increases, and finally screams. We're sorry to see that little creature screaming like that, maybe he's suffering. We would like to help him more than anything else. We also wish that infernal noise to stop! We have a headache and a tightening heart.

We really want to do something. But what?

Einstein's famous phrase comes to mind:

> *If I had only an hour to save the world, I would spend 55 minutes defining the problem well and 5 finding the solution.*

Here is exactly this the point. If we are in a room with a crying baby there are only two things to do: call mother's baby, understand the problem.

To be with him, to make funny faces, to sing songs we liked when we were young could not work. There can be a thousand reasons why that child does not stop crying: he might be hungry or overeating, he might be sleepy or not at all, be bored or so tired that he could not sleep, have a bad stomach, bad ears.

The mother can calm the baby more easily not only for a maternal ascendant, but above all because understands the reason for crying. For every case there is only one remedy.

It is a common experience to see a child scream and then mum solve everything simply by removing the bib or shoes or giving him that useless puppet on the high shelf.

Mothers' power, the power of how.

TELL ME WHO YOU ARE, I'LL GIVE YOU WHAT YOU NEED

As we have just seen in the example of the crying baby, if you do not understand what your interlocutor wants and what he needs, you will not be able to satisfy the question; you will continue to chase all the people (wrong) and lose a lot of time and money.

The first point is therefore *to know*.

Many companies completely skip this passage because they think only of their own point of view. For example, those who sell cheap cars believe that everyone is happy to save money on the car. But it is not true.

A person with a medium to high income, a person who has just obtained a promotion, or even a person with a medium / low income convinced that by buying a cheap car will have higher maintenance costs, he might think otherwise.

Now let's imagine that a car dealership has economic, second-hand and luxury cars. His "target" clearly includes different types of people. How does one of his salespeople know how to talk to the first customer who walks into the shop?

Probably you will rely on some signs: clothing, the car with which the customer arrived, if he has a family with children or single, if he is accompanied by a secretary or a friend, etc. And the salesman will surely ask a lot of questions.

The potential customer's answers will be used not only to understand what he is looking for (luxury or economic car) but also to understand how to manage the negotiation better.

Online is not so different. There are so many signals, data, that our potential customer not consider, during each step that brings him to our product and service.

To understand this step, we must once again consider all the progress Google has made in delivering relevant results. In other words, we and Google do or should do the same job: to understand for what purpose our client is moving.

The intent of a potential car buyer could be "to save on gasoline" or it could also be sensitiveness to the environment. Knowing this makes it different.

MOBILE REVOLUTION

"I do not have a laptop. I do everything with the smartphone. It's important to me, because I turn off notifications and use one application at a time. I only have one open app, and I can really focus on what's ahead of me instead of all the things that would come if I used a laptop" – Jack Dorsey, CEO of Twitter

Numbers say it all: 96% of people use the smartphone to search the net; 87% use it as the first search solution; today's top retailers generate almost half of their mobile sales, with a growth of 29% from year to year; 177 are the minutes spent every day on your mobile; 150 are the times when the smartphone is consulted every day; 9 seconds on average of a consultation on the net.

Statistics also say that 90% of users are not sure of which smartphone brand will buy when the search begins; 82% of smartphone users consult their phone in the store before making a purchase; 2 out of 3 users check their smartphone to find out more about an ad they've seen on TV; 1 in 3 users buy from a different business or brand from what they had in mind when they started the search.

The relationship with mobile, with your smartphone, is more than a fashion, has become now an experience, a consolidated habit, a change of mentality, *mobile mind shift*, which companies must consider by changing their marketing strategies.

Being able to access information, services and mobile news is not just a technical detail but a new way of approaching the world. People are much more likely to encounter products and services, but they also have specific needs: clarity, speed, fun, not having to overload devices.

It is no longer a matter of a moment when one puts oneself to the PC to look for something, but of the awareness and the expectation of finding answers at any moment.

Right here is the great news and opportunity: the smartphone in hand, information with a touch, lead people to look for not only what they need at that time, but the first thing that comes to mind.

Another change emphasized by mobile is that people have become so used to obtaining information that they have become dependent on it, regardless of the subject of the question and need.

People ask what the weather will be like tomorrow, which restaurant offers the best vegetarian menu, how to buy a house or which name is more suitable for the puppy ... everything is researched.

The relationship that people have now developed with the web and search engines is like a personal consultant, a trusted friend, always at hand.

Greater relevance has meant that research has increasingly become a personal issue. In other words, people no longer look for "something that is best for" but "what is best for them".

In the last two years research "for me" has increased by over 60%; those that start with "should I", on mobile, have even increased by 80%.

The aspect that follows is that we are in an era of high customization. In fact, research regarding the position increases in the same way.

In the car market for example, research with more activities is today: "auto parts near", "tire shops near", "car wash close to", "oil change close to" (entrepreneurs take note: do they answer these questions or are they investing a lot of money to try to scale the SERPs for "auto parts"?).

MOMENTS THAT MATTER

We said that people surf mobiles up to 150 times a day for a total of about 177 minutes: it is a lot of sessions and short duration; what Google has defined micro moments.[9] They are not all the same and everyone has a meaning and only one answer to give.

Summarizing we can identify 4 types:

---

[9] https://www.thinkwithgoogle.com/intl/it-it/risorse-di-marketing/micro-momenti/

I-want-to-Know Moments
I-want-to-Go Moments
I-want-to-Do Moments
I-want-to-Buy Moments

In moments I-want-to-Know, which occur at any stage of the day, users have an exploratory attitude: they are not online to buy (at least for now) but are looking for information or seek answers to their curiosity.

In I-want-to-Go moments, the buying intention is closer: users look for (82%) for a nearby store or business. Finding yourself that these moments are a great advantage: considering this, georeferenced research is strategic.

In moments I-want-to-Do the user is looking for immediate help to try something new or try to do something. This moment can precede or follow the purchase and is largely connected to the use of video: more than 100 million hours of "how-to" content were viewed in North America only in 2015.

In moments I-want-to-Buy users are ready to make a purchase and may need help deciding what and how to buy.

Knowing on which "moment" is your potential customer is therefore definitely an advantage, because it allows you to differentiate the way you propose to your target: appearing on Maps in Google results, providing tutorials on YouTube, showing ads and reviews relevant to choose, giving information that satisfy or increase curiosity.

We must guard the micro-moments and be quick to cover the areas.

Many companies think that it's just being there when people are with a credit card in hand or ready to buy. It is not like that.

Google uses an emblematic phrase that explains the situation well: "Moments that decisions are made, and preferences are shaped".

The second part of the sentence highlights a great opportunity: to be there when decisions are made, even if they were future decisions.

To understand these simple data:

- Users happy with the mobile experience tend to buy in the future (said by 9 out of 10 people interviewed)
- On the other hand, when people have a bad mobile experience, there is only a 60% chance of buying in the future
- "Neutral" experiences, that is, not bad but not good, are negative factors for the purchase and the recommendation to friends
- When people search on their smartphones they are 2, 3 times more likely to buy than when they browse in a store or even when they surf from a PC
- People who choose a store through a mobile search tend to spend around 10% more

Being in the moments that relies is therefore a fundamental competitive advantage. Especially if the competitors are losing it.

PART TWO: MARKETING IS BEFORE WEB MARKETING

WHEN IT WAS ENOUGH TO BE THERE

In the early days of the advertising era it was quite easy: it was enough to communicate the existence of a service or product, to state its goodness or usefulness, and it was enough.

"If goods are advertised effectively, persistently and widely in mediums circulating in the dealer's community, there is non denying that a tremendous demand can be created. This fact is too well-known to need illustration." – Marketing Methods and Salesmanship, 1914

Spread the message meant also make known the product..

It makes us smile today, for example, to see terms with which the bitter Fernet[10]introduced on a Milanese newspaper of 1865 its amazing virtues: "Febrifugal, vermifuge, tonic, corroborant, calefacient and anticoleric, can be taken with vermouth, into coffee, wine or broth, water, vinegar etc. It facilitates digestion, prevents nerve's irritation and opens appetite in a wonderful way. It is amazing for healing in just a few hours any malaise produced by spleen, heart disease, not to mention that stomach ache and sore head caused by poor digestion and old age».

The first Barilla[10] brand was registered in 1910, and was limited to represent a small, blond guy dressed in white-red-green with a

---

[10] A famous italian food company.

kitchen apron overturning the yolk of a huge egg in a cupboard full of flour, in front of the crowd of customers of the pasta factory; accompanying this image it was a simple text saying: "Barilla egg pasta". The elements that will make represent the identity of the Barilla brand are all there already - the eggs (which will later be incorporated into the logo still in use today), genuineness, Italian - there was no need to be persuasive or creative or allusive to exceed competitors: it was enough to say, "here we are".

The first advertisings were on the front pages of newspapers and magazines making it visible even for the illiterate (and in Italy, there were many ...). Soon they were joined by the wall advertising, with illustrated posters.

The surfaces of the cities, the walls, the spaces of means of transport become so crowded with messages, announcements and invitations, that already the author of the famous Italian novel Cuore, Edmondo De Amicis, described it as an unbearable invasion.

In the cosmopolitan Paris of the turn of the century it became impossible to drink a beer at the bar in peace, that "the advertising haunts you": you find it in your hand, on the cars that pass by, in the sky, on the table, on the back of the chair and even among the feet, on the sidewalk![11]

"There are in all corners thousand mouths that call you and thousand hands that beckon you. It is a network that wraps up all of Paris. And everything is cheap" – E. De Amicis

---

[11] Edmondo De Amicis, *Ricordi di Parigi,* 1879.

Maybe that was only a thing from abroad, from Industrial Revolution's countries, department stores, Universal Expositions and masses?

Not exactly. Even when getting into the carriages of public transport of modest Turin of 1899 De Amicis noted that "inscriptions and figures painted on the glass, hanging tags, notices of any shape and colour stuck to the sky and walls [want] at any cost, to make you get dressed, soaping and perfuming, making you change your home, take a newspaper pass and take a hydrotherapy treatment."[12]

What De Amicis was telling is a Turin horse-drawn tram from 1899. Is it so different today? I would say no.

Another Torinese by adoption and by exception, Italo Calvino, sixty years after De Amicis, thus photographed the extension "forest" of the poster invasion along the city's arteries: "On the sides of the highway, the children saw the forest: a thick vegetation of strange trees covered the view of the plain. They had fine, straight or oblique logs; and flat and extended hair, from the strangest shapes and from the strangest colours, [...] toothpaste, face, cheese, hand, razor, bottle, cow, tire, dotted with foliage of letters of the alphabet".[13]

In short, as they say, the landscape had become rather crowded.

But in the sixty years in between De Amicis and Calvino, advertising had not limited itself to expanding only from the streets to the motorways, it had also entered the houses. And with a megaphone in his hand.

[12] Edmondo De Amicis, *La carrozza di tutti*, 1899.
[13] Italo Calvino, *Marcovaldo*, 1963.

THE WAVE – IN

Starting radio broadcasts (in the '20s) and television (in the '30s), seize and exploit the opportunities for marketing channels was one step.

I finally said marketing (did you notice?), not advertisement or advertising, and not by chance: it is precisely in the early decades of the twentieth century, in the America of Ford, Singer and Coca Cola, that scholars place the statement of marketing as we understand it today. The first book reporting the word marketing on its title is 1914![14]

Without masses (of markets, of products, of consumers, of standardized needs, of tools), and without the consequent need to take care of the sale and not just the production, without market analysis, without an eye to the consumer ... well, at the beginning advertising was only enough.

"The ducks lay their eggs in silence. The hens instead cackle like crazy. What is the consequence? The whole world eats chicken eggs"
– Henry Ford

And indeed. The first radio advertisement in history was broadcast on August 28, 1922 on a New York station: Queensboro Corporation, a New York real estate company, paid $ 50 for a ten-minute message promoting apartment's sale in Jackson Heights. Not even 20 years passed and, again in New York, on July 1, 1941, just before the start of a baseball game (Brooklyn Dodgers vs.

---

[14] *Marketing Methods and Salesmanship* by Ralph S. Butler, H. De Bower, J. G. Jones.

Philadelphia Phillis) the first television advertising release was broadcast. It concerned a Bulova watch, it lasted 10 seconds and cost a total of 9 dollars (today a spot during the Super Bowl costs millions).

How many saw and heard that simple slogan "America runs on Bulova time"? Hard to say, it is estimated that at that time there were only 4000 TV sets in the New York area. But the future of TV was destined to more zeroes.

Even more than radio, television spread rapidly to the masses in the post-war world marked by the pursuit of well-being: in America TV sets were 3 million in 1950, 27 million in 1953 and 57 million in 1961. In 1968 almost, every American family had at least a television.[15]

In 1955 an Italian survey found that 370 thousand spectators watched TV in their own home, one million in the friend's home or relatives two or three times a week, two million and 300 thousand people watched TV shows two or more times a week in public places.

Enough to make your eyes glisten in the advertising world.

So here is the memorable start of Italian television advertising: on 3 February 1957, the Carosello broadcasts began, the public TV advertising space with its short, iconic and costly sketches (the companies paid them 1 million and five hundred thousand lire). For the record, the first Carosello in the history was sponsored by Shell.

But Carosello, with its format, was unique, and the Italian date that really interests us is another: a year before the closure of Carosello, in 1976, a ruling by the Constitutional Court breaks the RAI monopoly and opens the way to the private radio and TV stations,

---

[15] https://www.lacomunicazione.it/voce/televisione-a-storia/

first premises and then merged into national networks, financed by advertising investments.

Apart from the large national networks which catered for large companies, local broadcasters became immediately attractive for smaller businesses (retailers, SMEs, artisans) which could immediately advertise their product in their territory at a more affordable price.

From 1979 to 1985, television in Italy went from 6% to 35% of total advertising spend and growth continued to be strong until the end of 2000. It is the triumph of the industrial-television system, as defined by Seth Godin in the Purple cow: the lucrative circle advertising> distribution> increase in profit> purchase of new advertising space, which allowed the most aggressive companies to become giants.

And then? Then the system started having to deal with a new giant that, "surfing", arrived quickly on the crest of the wave.

"Switching to the radio and TV" was an opportunity initially but then it became a need.

It cost money of course. But the message arrived to many, possibly to everyone. It stuck in everyone's memory with its jingles. It resounded in the ear. It was part of everyday life (many hours, on average, those who spent in front of the TV). And it managed to generate profits very simply after all.

Since 1920, therefore, the fluttering hens of Fordian memory left the back yard and started laying their eggs on the sofa: "directly to your house, without additional charges".

But on this dense media network , voices and jingles, poultry and eggs, while economic and industrial progress have led the offer to grow up to demand and beyond, in an increasingly saturated market of products and almost satiated needs, while people have become increasingly busy and distracted or refractory, "be seen and heard", "squawking", is no longer enough: you have to "get noticed", stand out from the competition. Become a purple cow in a brown world.

Change focus. Aim for people. Interested. Convince them to choose. To buy.

The paths that the marketing world has travelled to survive this challenge still represent, in the digital era, marketing cornerstones, and have covered all four of the famous P (*product, price, promotion, placement*) of Mc Charty's marketing mix: the use of techniques of deep persuasion, construction of brand identity, creativity and innovation, price war, especially shift of attention from the object to the consumer-customer, the true keystone of today's world.

All these strategies have been put to the test by the last born of the media, that son of mass communication who, like so many mythological heroes, marked with his birth an attack of father's life: The Internet.

What is left and still works the old way of doing marketing? What was rethought? What has arrived again?

The network has become a new Big Apple, a new land of opportunities to seize, hens to place and eggs to sell.

But on the Internet, people have discovered that they want duck eggs. Because he could find them. And entrepreneurs have discovered that the right way to sell was no longer to make the voice of the hens, but of the customers.

AN OPINION MARKET

The first book reviews left on the Amazon website were decidedly critical. Initially reviews were written mostly by Amazon employees, who were encouraged to be honest by their employer. But how could they have the boss's permission to slag off those same products they were trying to sell? A bookseller sent a letter to Bezos enraged: did he know that his job was to sell books and not to throw them away?

Bezos, however, remained firm in his intuition of the need to overturn the perspective. According to him, the important one was not the good review of the book, but the service offered. It was not about making money selling things, it was about making money by helping customers make spending decisions. And customers would have trusted a lot more than the honest opinion of their peers than anything else, but at the same time they would probably have acted on their own.

Who was right, today is obvious.

When in September 2013 Guido Barilla told Radio24 that his company would never have made advertising that represented families other than traditional ones (or rather, traditionally associated with his Brand Image), Barilla found himself seriously in trouble. The statement circulated very fast on Twitter and Facebook, both in Italy and in the world, provoking protests and boycotts: even the cafeteria service of Harvard University decided to remove the Barilla pasta from its menu (in the US Barilla controls 30% of pasta market).

Guido Barilla apologized immediately and several times[16] but now the damage was done: a damage not so much economic (the campaigns of boycotting rarely affect the revenue directly) but a damage of reputation and image of the company, a damage of the brand.

"For a generation of customers used to doing
their buying research via search engine, a

---

[16] he sincerity of repentance was proven later by the numerous and concrete actions in favour of the LGBT rights implemented by the company.

company's brand is not what the company says it is, but what Google says it is." – Chris Anderson

---

The fact that companies can be seriously damaged by a social branding (eternal by the invincible memory of the Internet) was witnessed only a few months after the Barilla case by the speed with which the IAC, a major communication company that owns brands like Vimeo and Ask.com, fired his own employee for a racist tweet that virialized around the world on social networks. The girl had typed the unfortunate tweet in London before boarding a plane to South Africa and when she landed, she had discovered she had become famous despite herself and had been fired.

But do not be afraid: the good management of feedback and social media can also be a source of success for a company. When Chevrolet, in 2006, announced a competition in which people could create and propose an advertising film for the new company SUV, triggered the mockery of many marketers: as was obvious, many have uploaded online videos that massacred the product. The Chevrolet had taken this into account, accepted the comments and did not remove them: the SUV recorded a surge in sales and showed that in the age of the Internet the creation and control of advertising messages is less for marketing people than for users.

How can all these facts be explained?
Very simple: because "feedback" is among the things that have made the modern economy, as Tim Harford says. Because we live in the sharing economy, in the trust economy, and because Internet needs feedback to stand up.
The same algorithm of Google is based on the analysis of the feedbacks. When Larry Page and Sergey Brin started working on Google, they did nothing but translate a well-known concept into the academic world: the more an article is mentioned and the more authoritative it is.

The same, in a different form, characterizes every decision that people take on the web, continuously.

Many continue to see Google, or the web, and social media as different and distant things but are part of the same game.

Twenty years ago, when the Internet was just starting to take hold in our culture, forward-looking companies established their online presence in a world where they had a high degree of control. The interactivity and conversations were limited, the comments were a rarity and however the system was highly controllable and manipulee.

The birth of social networks, of the communities, meant that the game changed completely. A website is no longer a body, it cannot fail to consider what happens around, what users say.

In some ways we are experiencing an exasperation by feedback, but now we are so used that we can't do otherwise. And the ability to give and receive feedback is what keeps up the whole digital mechanism, social media, growing investments, every new idea that has overturned the world in recent years.

Amazon, Airbnb, Uber, have exploded precisely because of these factors: the possibility of having feedback on the service or asset that you intend to buy, the possibility of a place where such information is conveyed and amplified every day.

A NICHES MARKET

We cited Amazon for its customer-centred vision and its function as a review aggregator, but there is another lesson that can be learned from Bezos company: the fact that in the digital market the old 80/20 ratio (20% of products make 80% of sales) is completely skipped. In aggregate markets (so to speak, Amazon, iTunes, Zalando, etc.), it is not the Hit that makes the most of sales, but that immense 98% of niche products that maybe sell only one unit a month.

It is what Chis Anderson has defined the theory of the "Long Tail" and that allows us to define new immense opportunities:

"And then there's the Web. Forget it as a marketplace of products, and instead think of it as a marketplace of opinion. It's the great leveler of marketing. It allows for niche products to get global attention. Most products will be sold offline, much as they always were. But in the years to come, more and more products will be marketed online, taking advantage of the ability of Web methods to fine-slice consumer groupsand influence word of mouth more effectively than ever before in history. Not all industries lend themselves to an infinite variety of products, but all industries have an infinite variety of customers. Finally we can treat them like the individuals they are. It's the sunset of the thirty-second spot."[17]

MARKETING IS STILL BEFORE WEB MARKETING

Ten or even twenty years ago, a company with an online website was quite rare and could reap the rewards of a first mover with a relatively small investment.

Those who invested in digital, "the first banners", always declared themselves happy with the investment. Online advertising was cheap compared to today, because it was considered a secondary form, the

---

[17] Chris Anderson, *The long tail.*

public was not yet so large, and advertisers were not yet so many and confident.

In 2017, advertising in digital channels exceeded that in traditional channels. A shop without a website and the main social channels is a rarity. Everyone can and do everything.
For what we are saying, it does not matter if it's good or bad. What is important is the overcrowding that results from it. To be clear: in 2011, an average brand could expect an organic coverage of 26% on content posted on Facebook. Today that number is less than 1%.
Everyone is communicating, everyone has access to the same channels, the same technology, the same data, the same means.
This does not mean that the opportunities are not there but only that we must find a different path. Pay more attention. Diversify. Give predominance to strategy, to ideas rather than resorting to tactics.
Opportunities are there but we need to ponder with even more attention and spend well their ideas, their time, their money.
You cannot look in only one direction. You cannot just think of opportunities and you cannot believe those who say it's so easy...
The entrepreneur who wants to see results in the digital world must have the clarity to look at the picture, understand the potential but not distort the managerial spirit that has brought him to this point. Web marketing, called generically, is marketing applied in the digital world, it is not a discipline that cancels and invents all over again.

The new approach is not dictated by "being online" but by changing people's habits, in a clearly new era marked by technology.

"Today it is important to be present, but above all to be relevant and to add value" – Nick Besbeas

---

It is therefore good to imagine a blank sheet where to insert some items on either side of the sheet.

On one hand the opportunities, on the other the complexity, the critical points.

Opportunities are first and foremost in communicating in a personalized way: ad hoc messages for well-defined people and in well-defined moments.

The critical aspects lie precisely on this: identifying one's own audience (not the world) and achieving it in a relevant way.

Recapitulating: before web marketing, marketing comes first, again.

POSITIONING IN THE DIGITAL AGE

In 1955, while the Dove soap ad was being created, David Ogilvy discovered that its formula contained a "¼ of cream", as the famous words go. With a stroke of genius, Ogilvy took advantage of the ingredient to give the product a new sense and a new target: it was not just a soap that only cleaned, but a product of beauty and self-care for women with dry skin. "*I could have positioned Dove as a detergent bar for men with dirty hands*" – he will say later – *but chose instead to position it as a toilet bar for women with dry skin.*".

This is the most famous among the first examples of *positioning*, which Ogilvy defined in a very simple and concrete: "Positioning – This curious verb is in great favor among marketing experts, but no two of them agree what it means. My own definition is *what the product does and who it is for.*".[18]

---

[18] *Ogilvy on advertising*, from which the previous note is also taken.

However, if today positioning has become the most important and used marketing strategy, it is due to the job done in the seventies by exceptional thinkers such as Al Ries and Jack Trout. The two gave the following definition of the concept: "Positioning starts with a product. A piece of merchandise, a service, a company, an institution, or even a person. Perhaps yourself. But positioning is not what you do to a product. Positioning is what you do to the mind of the prospect. That is, you position the product in the mind of the prospect".[19]

Since then and for a very long time, a person with a minimum of familiarity with marketing, or even an entrepreneur with a pinch of strategy, could not think of positioning other than looking for differentiation and the reason why his product could stay or not stay on the market.

What does a product do, why it differs from the market, how it communicates its advantages and differences, who it is addressed to, who are these people...? Even the business plans started consciously from here, from the idea of differentiating, of having an idea, of defining a strategy.

At a certain point, almost suddenly, we found ourselves talking about something else and in another way. The term positioning now leads more to Google's SERP than to the brand concept.

People focus so much on positioning on Google search pages that it has become paradoxical: the term has lost every bit of strategic thinking and planning.

Even in Italy, agencies have been promoting the idea that it is enough to be first (on Google) to then be bought. And similarly, by analogy and contamination, started just to be on Facebook, just be

---

[19] *Positioning: The Battle for Your Mind*

visible, have a lot of fans, have an *influencer* that shows you to his audience.

Quickly, we have reached a point where we are positioned on a channel to show off. With two results:
– show off, be seen, which today is very difficult;
– but without demonstrable results, you have not achieved anything.
The result can make you laugh, but can also make you cry: companies, driven by this crazy idea, pushed by inexperienced marketing agencies, or unethical, spend a lot of money to get back nothing.
With the same argument we could explain why so many people today continue to say, "the internet does not work!"

POSITIONING IS TWICE MORE IMPORTANT TODAY

The paradox is that positioning, in the original concept, is of an extreme importance today.
The great changes we have seen in the previous pages have in fact led to a single judge and a single yardstick: the client and the relevance.

The challenge today is not to be seen, to have a website and to push people onto it, but to preside over a channel where we expect our target client to arrive. The challenge is always the same: to choose if our soap is for women who want to take care of their hands or for the mechanic who must wash them after work.

Then – and this is the new key challenge– to understand what are his/her real needs. What they talk about, how they talk, how much they usually spend on soap, whether they're vegan or crazy steak eaters, on what device they surf, at what time, for how long.

It may seem like an enormous and tedious task – I do not say that it is not in a sense – but there are two fundamental things at stake:

1. communicate in a relevant way;
2. sell your own product (for real).

These are not new concepts, except for the enormous amount of data we have, but they are all there is to know and do.

When in the agency we thought of a new name for our approach, we deliberately thought of a name that would combine the words *search*, *marketing* and *design*.

We think that we cannot communicate and sell in the digital world without these three things:

- *search*
- *marketing* (understood as study, strategy, positioning)
- *design* (intended as a design that starts from an idea to make it concrete, tailor-made).

The ready-made ideas, the fast tactics, the ones that come from America... that all I do not want to say is wrong, but it's not for your client and therefore not for your company.

First, we reason and then we decide what to do. First you know and then you decide. The sooner you have a plan, the better.

" Why are you running if you're not on the right track?" – German proverb

---

MARKETING: COST OR INVESTIMENT?

An entrepreneur who wanted to advertise his business in the 90s (it still happens today) met an advertising agency, which created the message, the message was displayed on billboards in the middle of the street or broadcast on television and seen by a lot of people.

The pitch started and closed with a prediction: we estimate that "by passing every day an amount of people …"

Even the television data had this type of problem: a thousand people watching a program may have decided to go to the bathroom or prepare a sandwich at the time of the spot.

There was no guarantee or completely reliable method to evaluate the ROI of a project. In a sense, "hope" was the only strategy.

Today "hope" should not be among the options and should not even appear in the vocabulary of a marketing agency, as well as of the entrepreneur.

It's time to know. The data help us in all phases of the process: to make smarter decisions, to evaluate the effectiveness of our actions, to determine the result.

As for the result, however, the situation is more complex and is one of the other great challenges of digital marketing.

MARKETING RESPONSIBILITY: WHAT TO EXPECT?

" The goal of marketing is to make sure that customers know, appreciate and trust you " –
Anonymous

We have always talked about the relationship between marketing and sales, whether marketing is sales, whether it is a part of sales or the opposite. In other words, the question is whether marketing sells or not. And over the years the answers have changed to a great extent.

The keyword that every advertising consultant has used thousands of times is "investment": *it is not a cost, but an investment!*

Yes, it is certainly an investment, but investments, by definition, provide some characteristics such as: risk, percentage of success, profit and loss.

The problem of marketing has always been this: its importance but also its lack of responsibility.

Today it is different, or at least it should be.

The entrepreneur who implements a digital marketing plan has a great advantage over his colleagues in the past: he has data available and the data do not lie.

There is a cost, there is a ROI, a return on investment.

Simple, no? It seems so but it is not so much.

THE ROI OF DIGITAL MARKETING

One of the big problems is understanding what a "right return" means.

Did a campaign to increase brand awareness and generate sales, likes, and referrals work?

For a twentieth century entrepreneur, probably not. For a marketer of this century, yes, for an entrepreneur today ... let's say yes and no.

Who's right? Let's dig a little before we understand better what we're talking about.

Following the classical interpretation, the ROI of a web project would be easily determinable. The profit is calculated as the sales generated as a result of a specific action (which can be monitored), the expenses incurred are deducted, the return on the investment is made. We are happy or sad according to the result.

But the situation is more complex. Today the meaning of "return on investment" needs to be rethought.

A profit in the short term, driven by an exceptional promotion, by an activity pushed on the target, by retargeting, by flooding the web with ubiquitous and difficult to close banners, by the intervention of an influencer of the sector, may not be the best thing. For example, it could scratch the brand identity (positioning) and make a much larger loss in the long run.

On the other hand, an activity aimed at consolidating positioning may not have immediate effects on sales.

For example, according to Google data, people who visit a site that satisfies them, especially from smartphones, declare that they will buy the product or service as soon as they need it. Over the 67% and 80% recommend to friends and relatives that specific company even if they have not purchased. Therefore, we have left the idea of classical positioning, but this is an experience aimed at strengthening the relation with the market. Positive experience, but that we cannot immediately measure in economic terms.

But we can know what kind of experience the users of our site have had and what we can expect. We can evaluate time of stay, feedbacks, social signals, even where our users' eyes are addressed and how much they have been taken from our message.

This is a ROI and it is no coincidence that we speak of ROI for a long time as *Return on Impression*.

Another type of ROI is that of acquiring a client through an action of SEO and search. But it is so emblematic that we can summarize two scenarios:

- In the first case, a consulting company asks that more people visit their site;
- In the second case, another company asks users to visit an e-commerce.

We are coming to the solution …

Imagine two companies which both spent 100 and then had 100 people visiting their website, you'd say they both spent one unit per visitor. But If the *converted* visitors spent 100 and 50 in each cases, the ROI are 0 and −50 eg very different.

In both cases the results can not satisfy the managers of the two companies and would seem to agree with those who say that marketing is a necessary cost.

However, this is clearly a partial view.

If the consulting firm's clients bought a home loan service, it could be a sporadic sale and one could only hope for the virtuosity of referrals. If they purchased an accounting service and are professionals, they clearly have another meaning. We must therefore remember that the value of a buyer is not given by his single first purchase, but by all the potential purchases he will be able to make in the future.[20]

> *" The greatest asset of a company is represented by its customers, because without customers there are no companies " –*
> *Michael LeBoeuf*

It now becomes clear that:

- You cannot know the ROI of your marketing activity if you do not know how much your customer is worth.
- You cannot know the ROI of your marketing activity if you do not know how it affects the customer satisfaction on their company's growth.
- You cannot know the ROI of your marketing activity if you do not know exactly what happens if that customer is not acquired but chooses a competitor.
- You cannot know the ROI of your marketing activity if you do not know how much the competitors are spending for the same customer.
- You should not do any marketing activity if you do not have the slightest idea of the above points.

In short, taking Paul Samuelson's words:

> *If you want some excitement, take some money and go to Las Vegas.*

---

[20] We are clearly talking about *Lifetime Value* (LTV), an "indicator that measures predictable profits based on the relationship with customers, starting from their buying behaviour over time" (Wikipedia)

IN MARKETING, HOPING IS NOT AN OPTION

For a long time, the advertising world, when it was still called in that way, was based on a creativity almost voluntarily unconstrained by rules. I gave a creative guru some time to think and he would come up with a slogan or a campaign to be able to get noticed.

The challenge was to show up, to get noticed.

"To be seen" was based on a very simplistic idea of business world: if nobody knows, you do not sell anything; as a result, more, people know your product or service and more chances are that it can be purchased.

Countless agencies and consultants have worked using Ford's famous phrase: "Ducks lay their eggs in silence. The hens instead cackle like crazy. What is the consequence? The whole world eats chicken eggs."

So, the winning recipe seemed to flutter as loud as possible and stronger than the others. On the other hand, it was said, if you don't do it, then one of your competitors will.

Over the time, with more people willing to shout about their own merchandise, even at the beginning of the digital age, the need and the approach have changed slightly.

It was no longer necessary only to be there, to scream loudest, but to do it with a certain skill and to be noticed among so many who did the same thing. We started talking about the "wow effect".

But that time no longer exists: with the amount of content and information accessible today, all this is not enough.

Even "getting noticed", being creative could not be enough anymore and in fact it is no longer enough. The truth is that the digital world has completely changed the rules of the game, has made the customer really the supreme boss.

He is in a justly privileged position and the internet made him informed and skilled, so much to be able to choose regardless of the persuasive techniques and relying instead on his previous needs and experiences and/or the people who are close to him.

"There is only one supreme leader: the customer. The customer can fire everyone in the company, from the president down, simply by spending his money somewhere else" – Sam Walton, *fondatore di Wal-Mart*

The challenge today is completely new and different than in the past. We've talked about this before, it's about being *relevant*. And therefore *opportune*.
Do not try to communicate to everyone just for the sake of communicating, but to do it in the right way and at the right time and to the right people.
But first you must take a step back: know *why*. But also know *what*, *how*, *who*.

THE ERA OF DATA

" If you cannot measure, you cannot improve " – *Genichi Taguchi*

Without data you have no way of knowing if you are improving or getting worse. And it has also been said that what is measured is improved. But this is only half the story and we'll talk later.

First there is another aspect: the data is used to indicate the way before starting. If it is true that the important thing is *relevance*, if your customers expect relevance, how can you succeed if not based on reliable information?

All the main companies we know work like this. There are no secrets or spells to search and find. It's simpler than you think.

For example, airlines use real-time data to analyse the performance of their fleet, like other transport companies. They use data to make decisions about flights and departures. They use the data to customize the experience of each individual customer. The promotions we see on specialized sites, periodic promotions, bonuses and incentives we love so much are always the result of data, knowledge and understanding.

A recent *Harvard Business Review* study centred the question to perfection: we analysed the fact that the real challenge was to identify opportunities and make smart, reasoned decisions.

Let's make a small digression to understand us better: the data say that many (40%) of people who buy items for children do not have children, but they make the purchase only to bring a gift to friends and relatives.

Not knowing this data is the reason why most of the advertising is addressed to potential customers by saying "for your child...", hoping that for your child you do not mind spending or suspend any critical judgment.

The *Harvard Business Review* study involved 646 executives, managers and professionals from all industries in the world and noted that many companies are integrating data acquisition and analysis into their decision-making processes.

This research highlights an obvious contrast and creates new questions. Why when you handle a company you rightly claim to make decisions based on data but when it is about marketing it is not so based on data, but on the perception?

The answer lies in the lack of understanding of the opportunities we have and the lack of "responsibility" with which marketing in general must confront.

In other and simpler words: just hope and wait. Communication today must start from data, be monitored and judged based on data, and defined as "good or bad" based on more data.

So, welcome to the age of data, listening to people, marketing that takes responsibility. And entrepreneurs who make smart decisions.

"We have to move from the numbers that hold the score to the numbers that run the best actions" –
David Walmsley

PART THREE: DESIGN AND STRATEGY

ASKING THE RIGHT QUESTIONS

Even today I happen to be asked whether it is better to open a shop on the road or an e-commerce: it is a question that betrays all the confusion that exists in marketing.

The problem lies in wanting to run before being able to walk, having answers before asking the right questions, looking for a shortcut before knowing the goal.

In other words: if you do not know what your goal is, who your customers are, how they are used to buy, what they are really looking for, every tactic is bound to fail.

"The client expects you to have knowledge of their stuff, not just your stuff " – Jeffrey Gitomer

---

Returning to the question "better a physical store or an e-commerce?" I have another observation that should always be made: someone will buy my products? And why?

For me it is a concept of fundamental importance: before doing online marketing, you must have clear marketing, before thinking of positioning your brand on digital channels, on the SERP of Google, we need to place the brand in consumer's minds.

Continuing with the "bizarre" requests, especially in the early years of our activity, we were asked to develop a site like Amazon or Groupon! If in some ways it was feasible, with the right budget or with a few tweaks, however it would not have achieved the same results, clearly.

Similarly, often I happen to hear entrepreneurs disappointed because their products are not bought and they blame the internet for it.

It is clear if you then go peek on their websites and you realize that they sell a product twice as expensive than Amazon, that the delivery service is inadequate or that there are plenty of negative reviews on that particular product or brand.

It seems so trivial to use this book to say these things, but clearly it is not a concept so obvious. Marketing is not a "thing" that can fix all the problems of a business, but to enhance its virtue. It is the art or science of meeting the right question with the right offer.

If you have a product or service that lives up to expectations, then in this case being online in the right way and at the right time makes the difference.

That's exactly why giants like Google, Amazon, Groupon have been and are so successful. It is not distribution, global advertising that makes them so reliable, but it is the concept behind it, the entrepreneurial idea that is relevant to its audience.

"The marketing's enemy is hit and run selling, where the goal is to sell at all costs, instead of acquiring a long-term customer" - Philip Kotler

---

A manager should start with the following questions:

• Are we up to market?
• Why should customers choose us rather than a competitor?
• What is the winning factor of my products or services?
• What is the strongest need/desire of my clients?
• How do my competitors answer these questions?

These questions are the basis for starting a positioning approach. Losing a bit of time in answering has the same meaning as wasting time on tying shoes before a run; you will leave a second later, but you will avoid falling after a few meters.

THE RIGHT QUESTIONS BEFORE YOU RUN

Let's see how the answer to these questions can have an impact on online presence.

Are we up to the market?

Imagine the case of an e-commerce. One of the frequent problems is that people visit the website but leave the page without concluding the purchase. Traffic (how many people arrive at the site) is certainly important, but it is not, as one might mistakenly think, the most important factor.

If every day 100 people arrive but only buy in 2 (the numbers are examples, in some cases it could be an excellent return), one of the reasons could be "convenience". One of the mistakes that many entrepreneurs make is to approach the digital without having to deal with the digital.

For example, almost everyone offers online prices that are more advantageous than in the store. Others are confident because they offer the most advantageous prices on the territory. But communicating and selling online presupposes completely different rules. Both in terms of opportunities but also in terms of competition.

When online the references are those of the web: this means entering competition with stores in other countries or continents.

Not only the price counts, but the reliability, timing, reputation and strength of the brand must always be evaluated.

One of the things that must be understood, especially today with digital evolution, is that it is not about getting as many "passers" as possible to increase the possibility of being chosen.

It is about being *congruent* on the market and *relevant* for its customer.

Indicate who they are and what they are really looking for is the next step.

Why should customers prefer me and not a competitor? What is the winning factor of my products or services?

Differentiation is at the basis of marketing and business. In the online world it's more important the more complicated. With so much offer and competition, it seems almost impossible to find something really differentiating. Find something unique? Even more difficult.

Especially online, we need to think differently. Nobody pretends that your company is unique in all respects or has a unique product. If so, and if the product was valid, you would be in a monopoly regime and you would not have problems.

Knowing why users should buy in your store is something more complex and if we want less tangible.

Unless your company has patented technology, it is likely that competitors will have at least similar products.

What really matters is not how unique you are, but how much people think about it.

Consider some of the leading car brands. Mercedes has an instantly recognizable logo and is, in many people's minds, a symbol of status and success. This does not mean that a Mercedes is built in a fundamentally different way from a Honda or a Toyota and still no other car's brand has the same connotation.

Even the way you do business can become a distinctive and discriminating factor for the buyer. The online retailer Zappos (in Italy we can think of Zalando) is widely known and used because it offers not only free shipping but also free returns without any charges. In other words, what you are inclined towards buying has to do with customer service.

> *"Winning companies also turn their customers into winners. The most experienced companies constantly create new customer value, are deeply customer oriented and satisfy their needs" - Philip Kotler*

These analyses therefore lead us to reflect not only on "what you sell" but also on "how you sell it". We are therefore talking about customer experience, *user experience* in terms of usability of the online channel, ease of use, compatibility and enjoyment via mobile.

For example, statistics reveal that:

• Users satisfied with the mobile experience tend to buy in the future (9 out of 10 people interviewed);
• On the other hand, when people have a bad mobile experience, there is a 60% less chance of buying in the future;
• "Neutral" experiences, are negative factors for the purchase and the recommendation to friends;
• When people search on their smartphones it is 2.3 times more likely that they will buy compared to when they are browsing inside a store or even when they are surfing from a PC;
• People who choose a store through a mobile search tend to spend around 10% more.

Why am I mentioning this data? Because being unique and having a strong reason to be preferred today can also be represented by how you are communicating and how you can enjoy your online mobile content.

Doing marketing and doing online marketing is always clear that there is only one supreme judge: your client, the user.

What is the strongest need/desire of my clients?

This is the central point in my marketing plan, and it is no coincidence that *data driven* is one of the expressions that always leads my business' approach in Search Marketing Design.

To explain this better I'd like to quote a very famous movie: "What Women Want" with Mel Gibson.

In the opening scenes, short of ideas and looking for inspiration, Mel starts to use the products (lipstick, socks, and other female accessories) himself to try to understand which is the right message to convey. It doesn't work. He therefore strives to "reason as a woman" and begins to imagine an advertisement of a beautiful woman in a bikini on the beach... At that point he realizes that he is still thinking like a man.

The turning point is when, due to a short circuit, it gets the power to really listen to the thoughts of women. Only at this point every message will be the right one.

The film is widely used in the marketing world to explain the challenge of insiders and entrepreneurs to communicate in the right way and therefore understand the needs, dreams that are the basis of purchases.

How do my competitors answer these questions?

Analyse, study the market, find out what the competitors are doing, what is working for them and where they are losing opportunities: this is also the basis of a marketing plan that is respected, and it is also here that there are the greatest opportunities for a company.

A NEW APPROACH FOR NEW TIMES

We need to think strategically and in the digital world this is equivalent to having a broad view that translates, in practice, into a multi-channel strategy.

At one time, as we have seen, it was reasonable and profitable to spend a certain amount of money to position themselves in a SER.

Today, however, people come to our products in a completely different way: varied, fragmented.

Two surprising statistics that I think are emblematic: most people search online for a product or service without knowing the main brand they want to buy. Every day on Google there are new searches, words and phrases never typed before (16%). It means that we are moving towards an unexplored territory where the only thing to do is try to be *relevant*.

Understanding who and what he is looking for, why he is looking for it, what is the preferred mode of dialogue, what is the experience that most satisfies him. All this clearly goes beyond SEO, search, social media, content marketing, web design and the same user experience.

To keep up with the digital customer, we need to think like the digital customer: more oriented towards the result than the path. Taking again the example of the film by Mel Gibson mentioned earlier: you cannot put yourself in the shoes of a woman reasoning as a man!

Today the approach, the overview counts far more than the single tactic. What's the point of being first on Google when most users will never buy your product?

And if that happens, what's the reason? How can the route be reversed?

The only way to do this is to follow the customer on his purchase path. A path that is completely different from 5 years ago.

When we talk about Search Marketing Design we refer to: a new model for completely new times and dynamics.

In the chapter "Research Psychology" we have already seen some important innovations, as for example the furniture has influenced the relationship between customer and company. More generally, however, the whole path that goes from the acquisition of information to the purchase has changed.

A way to understand the complexity is to highlight Dave Chaffey's best-selling "Digital Marketing"; a simple but effective text, which is also used in specialist university courses.

Dave explains that to understand digital marketing and to have an effective and profitable online presence, 5D (Digital devices, Digital platforms, Digital media, Digital data, Digital technology) must be kept in mind.

Devices: the audience interacts with smartphones, tablets, desktop computers but also via TV and gaming platforms.

Platforms: most interactions take place through browsers or apps like Google, Facebook, Youtube, etc.

Media: search engines, social media, social messaging, mail, etc.

Data: all this leads to the possibility of collecting a wealth of valuable data for companies. For the main players as well ad for small businesses.

Technology: the technology used to make an experience more or less significant.

Now, if we focus only on one of these "D" we can certainly have luck, but it is not possible to maximize the result and we are always in the unfortunate situation of waiting and hoping; or, "share and pray" referring to unconditional trust in content and social marketing.

A different approach instead:

- It starts from the data to get to know your audience
- Draw a personalized message: in content and use
- Choose channels (media) intelligently

- Optimize your budget by focusing only on what the data indicate to be relevant
- Monitor and test, or collect data continuously (personalized this time on your market and your company) to continuously optimize your impact
- Awareness of the efforts and goals achieved

Now it should be clear what we mean by new approach. All that remains is to start creating plans for Search Marketing Design. To take advantage of data, make smart decisions, get better results.

And stop spending a lot of money unnecessarily.

HOW TO CHOOSE THE RIGHT PARTNER

While I was writing, I heard a little voice saying: "Why talk about marketing if someone else has to do it?"

I answer as if someone had really asked for it: the purpose of this book is to make the reader, the entrepreneur or the marketing and commercial director think about the dynamics we are experiencing and regulate the online market and beyond.

So, also by acquiring some information "from insiders", we can really create a well-structured and effective plan, or we can choose who to be helped. The pages of this book are intended as a reference point for the selection, definition and monitoring of objectives. Because marketing, is this: to set goals, measure them, reach them.

When we talk about "promoting" products and services, almost everyone is convinced that we can do it ourselves or we can have something to say. Mistaken? Not necessarily.

In some ways every entrepreneur should have a healthy passion for marketing, know well the concepts, and drive his business in the right direction.

Realistically, however, in the complexity of the dynamics of the digital market, this means knowing how to choose the right partners.

Of course today there is so much literature on the subject, that it may not seem necessary to have a professional, but it is clear that it can only be true in certain cases and in certain measures. If you are a freelancer, if you are the only person on the team, it may make sense to do marketing in the first person. In other cases this is not always the case: it may be wiser to find a team of experts in the field.

AGENCY OR FREELANCE?

The web and its global market makes it possible to find competent professionals with excellent references all over the world, and it is easy to find competences and services at a good price in India, the Philippines, or some other so-called "developing countries".

The idea of working with freelancers is therefore recurrent and also has some excellent motivation. Some of the best professionals in the digital world are freelance by choice, they are called "digital nomads".

However, there are some aspects to think about:

- Marketing is so vast that the skills required are now many and varied;
- The user's journey is so fragmented that to meet and talk to him requires many tools and skills;
- Many freelancers are extremely specialized only in one or a few disciplines.

Very often when you think of freelancers you always think in economic terms: you think it can be convenient to hire a person, maybe young, rather than hire an agency with a shop on the road.

And many think of freelancing as a stage between do-it-yourself and working with an agency.

In most cases a freelance will be a good choice, but you will have to hire a whole team, coordinate them, follow them, make them speak the same language.

I know companies that have hired freelancers to find other freelancers and think about all this, but clearly it does not seem to be such a rational choice in terms of time, resources and outcomes of the project.

Not because I'm biased, but because a company has to find a team ready and trained: this is why I find that working with an agency is still the best choice.

The following question is: which agency is really needed for my business? How to choose it?

HOW TO CHOOSE A WEB MARKETING AGENCY?

Regarding choosing a web marketing agency, the analogies are wasted: it's like getting married, hiring a trusted collaborator, choosing a partner, as easy as finding a needle in a haystack …

Yes, it's not simple.

However, if the entrepreneur becomes the protagonist of this choice and dedicates a pinch of time and attention, things can be simpler and ensure better results. Here are some points that I consider fundamental and can be a short guide to choosing the ideal collaboration.

Starting with why (again)

Why are you looking for an agency to promote your business? Why do you think and are you convinced to do marketing? What are the reasons and expectations that are at the base?

These "abstract" questions will lead to very specific and concrete needs: for example, awareness of a brand identity and positioning problem, a neckline between the online and offline world, a lack of presence in Google's SERP or on social media, the desire to promote an online purchasing process, the need to increase margins for certain products, etc.

Choose the "type" of agency

By identifying priorities within your organization, you will save time and money on the journey.

One advice is to think for goals: make a list, choose 25, and leave only 5 (suggested by Warren Buffet). Finally, search the market for those who have the characteristics to ensure the achievement of those objectives.

The era of hybrid marketing (and "hybrid" agencies)

Last, but not least, it must be considered that today's market is not at all linear but rather complex, multifaceted, multi-channel, hybrid.

The hybrid marketing concept [21] s still confused and used in a generic way. An example could be that a marketing activity that includes two or more channels are used to reach the user, a similar definition to multi-channel marketing.

However, "hybrid", beyond the academic definitions, makes good the concept of uniting not only multiple channels (social, search, off line) but above all to think in this direction, making analog and digital converge: some physical stores, for example, put *url* in plain

[21] http://www.oxfordreference.com/view/10.1093/oi/authority.20110803095952529

view on the windows revolutionizing the way of doing business and communicate.

In such a situation it is anachronistic the expert who knows all about marketing and nothing digital, or vice versa. Today, marketers and marketing agencies must therefore have solid traditional foundations, and must be able to move with ease on new channels and in new ways.

There is not only execution (it will be done well or bad) but the sustainability and profitability of the project. To confirm this, just look at two emblematic factors: the marketing agencies that have always been recognized as leaders are now all hybrid agencies, where advanced technical skills mix perfectly with an equally solid know-how.

The most desirable professionals, according to recent surveys 22, are those who combine the famous "soft skills", the traditional theory with technical skills such as mastering social dynamics, programming, data analysis, etc.

More ideas and tips for choosing an agency

Many think that the choice of an agency is the purchase, or rather the rental, of execution and that only counts the performance. In fact it is about finding someone who really understands your story, your dreams and with whom you will be pleased to talk. For example, a marketing plan requires maximum transparency, in some ways it is like a doctor of trust. There is a need to really tell everything about the company, its products, its people, even the things that no one would put online or on a billboard; especially those. If the interlocutor is not in line with company values, it will almost never work. In everyday work it also means to contradict those who have chosen it to bring a real advantage to the company, really affecting growth and turnover. To be able to overcome even the physiological "frictions" there must be trust, empathy, a human factor.

As Jeffrey Gitomer says, I also do not believe in "I trust but I do not like it". The agency you choose should therefore have references and facts to trust, but also that spark that makes you say you will love working with her.

In addition to the human factor, there are also other criteria for choosing an agency. Objective criteria, for example how long it has been on the market, how many people work there, who has worked in the past, what case histories can present, which customers have similarities with your company, which specializations and awards can boast. Everything depends on the first point: your needs and priorities. An agency that has won the Oscar for advertising, which has the site named "most beautiful of the year", cannot count if its goal is to position itself as a leader on Google and increase e-commerce sales. Likewise, if you are aiming for internationalization, it does not matter if the people of the agency are nice but if they do not know how to speak English!

Trusting "your own kind"

When it comes to choosing an online marketing agency, the first thing to do is ask Google! It is not wrong, indeed. In some ways it is the first test: if for example I look for "SEO agency Milan" it is normal to give preference to those who are in the first places of the results, and it is equally normal to doubt SEO agencies that instead are buried like the famous skeletons in the wardrobes.

However, agencies that heavily sponsor their services may also appear in the results, making you believe that they are the right ones to pick, perhaps helped by slogans such as "customers right away" thus making you forget all the points we have talked about.

It will seem paradoxical, but in 2018, in the age of Artificial Intelligence, the very dear word of mouth is almost always the winning weapon. Word of mouth with humor, though! For example, today there is a confusion between reputation, reliability and visibility. Agencies that on the social media are undisputed protagonists, with pages that burst of likes and shares, could appear the right partner. I do not say that very social agencies are "bad", I suggest rather something that has always worked: "talk with your neighbors".

Take an hour to meet an old friend who has a business and get to know well with whom he worked and how he found himself (not only in terms of results, but also on the points discussed above). Or, this in Italy seems almost a sacrilege, check and speak with the testimonials that all the agencies present on their website.

And here's a last clarification, a bit of controversy: an element that if it is not a proof of the quality of the services offered, is more than a clue, it is the rate of redemption. If an agency has 1000 customers and only 5 are still current, some questions will have to be addressed.

Another aspect to consider is that a lot of work load, often of very large companies, is outsourced and fragmented among many other agencies. In other words: an agency that claims to have worked with Pirelli... could only have posted the posters in the city!

ANALYSIS

Data is not something abstract or nerd stuff. It is invaluable information that people continually offer about their dreams and needs. Inputs that companies can seize to be relevant.

About ten years ago, no one would have dreamed of talking about a business without having prepared a business plan, one of those documents in which information was exposed, justifying the choices and potential of the birth company. In recent years the philosophy of startups, *lean methods*, have instilled an excessive confidence in correcting company plans and have finally led to a real approximation and lack of preparation.

The same digital world, apparently so accessible, can bring companies without an adequate preparation to spend time and money, getting poor results.

All successful companies are characterized by intuitions, but above all by business studied and verified before being set up. It does not mean that there is no need on the job corrections , but it must be about improving adjustments and not about a continuous attempt of fate.

Search Marketing Design starts from the analysis of data: to create strategies that can produce results as they are drawn on reliable information, on a knowledge of both the market (traditionally understood) and the digital market.

The paradoxical thing is that the data are now accessible and copious and is therefore only a matter of will and method in collecting and examining them, to understand which ones are worth dwelling on.

Another important point is that data does not only offer a trace for online communication, but can be valuable allies to direct the company in the right direction.

Starting from data today is not just a possibility,
starting from data is a must!

Imagine having to buy a gift to a friend and go to a clothing store. We have a vague idea of what he likes, we probably have an orientation budget, we could also have an idea of the kind of gift we would like to make, for example a tie. But what kind of tie should we choose? Juvenile, serious, classic? What color?

Most probably we find ourselves quite confused and it is no coincidence that we often make sure that the shop allows a change. An excellent way to make a good gift, continuing our example, could then be to get more information to avoid mistakes and increase the chances that our friend is satisfied with the choice.

An almost infallible way could therefore be to call his wife and be advised. She will know what kind of ties he loves, what he already has in the closet and other details that surely escapes us and she will help us to make our friend a gift in line with his tastes and our idea and budget.

I am sure that each of us has used this perspicacity so many times and that everyone understands the importance of information before a choice.

This is what happens or should happen in marketing: having information to be truly relevant to customers.

With a big difference: when it comes to business there is no tie at stake and usually there is no possibility of getting back their investments.

THINKING *BEFORE* STARTING IS WORTHWHILE

"What is the use of running if you are not on the right track?" – German proverb

Greenpal is a well-known company in America that deals in lawn maintenance, a sort of Uber of gardening. Bryan Clayton, from the marketing team, started by promoting an advertising campaign to let its owners know about the Nashville owners. Landing pages were created and looked like a good slogan: "Lawn professionals are just a click away".

In theory everything was correct: in the area almost every house has a private garden and everyone wants to have a nice one, the ad appeared in almost all the SERP related to gardening and presented after a short time a percentage of clicks over 1 % and a conversion (customers) 10% higher.

A traditional company, not analyzing data, would be anyway satisfied - and the same would happen and it happens even in the absence of results, perhaps they would blame crisis or the Internet!

But Greenpal did something different, they analyzed the data available. They then realized that Nashville was largely populated by a working class, medium and low income, and therefore they would have been very sensitive with fees.

The new announcement was therefore written on the basis of this information: "The most economical lawn care in Nashville: starting at only $ 20"

The landing page was redesigned with the same cut and the results were not long to arrive: a 200% increase in clickthrough rate and a 30% increase in-page conversion.

Similar results are on the agenda for anyone adopting a data driven approach, which starts with the data. A job that might seem initially boring, nerd stuff, becomes an important moment for every company: understanding the right leverage, the characteristics of its market, how the competition moves, make smart decisions, better decisions.

CUSTOMIZATION AND RELEVANCE

The example of Greenpal may seem too simplistic and in some ways it is. In fact, it is not a question of using data only for the announcement of an online advertisement or for the slogan of a web page. The entire digital ecosystem, and not only that, must now be guided by data analysis.

"What helps people, helps businesses" – Leo Burnett

A recent Salesforce report determines the situation well:
"Ours is a culture forged by constant connections mobile access to everything imaginable, the instant we need it.
The result is that customers, consumers, patients, and citizens are supremely empowered with more information and choice than ever before, making it an even greater endeavour to sustain loyalty. As more and more data sources come online with the internet of things, we see many new possibilities (and complexities). As customers connected boundaries expand, expectations are likewise being elevated.
What does this mean for business? In short, these changes are creating an intelligence imperative both for companies serving consumers and those serving entire organisations. It s no longer enough for customer experiences to be simple and fast. Increasingly, customers expect every touchpoint to be personalised and proactive."

Each personalized contact means significant messages, in every channel, in every approach with the client, online as well as offline.
The customer is no longer willing to listen to standard messages, to be treated as a number, as part of a target.
So how can you offer personalized messages and services if you do not have the right information?

> *"To get the right message to the right person at the right time, you first need to get the right data at the right time"* – John Caldwell

The problem is not the availability of information, but the selection and use that companies make (or do not) of it.

To simplify, I suggest focusing on two main types:

1) Data that reveal information about your market
I think of a very widespread but undervalued tool, like Google AdWords. Most of the people work only with the control panel simply to understand how their campaigns are working but in fact it is a much more powerful tool than that. The costs for each query, for example, are an excellent indicator of what the operators are doing in a market and what people are looking for. Starting from here to analyze how the user's journey continues can lead to new, sometimes even cheaper and more profitable ways.
Another aspect which some think is too obvious to talk about (but experience tells me otherwise) is the volume of research for a given product or service. Too often I have heard entrepreneurs dissatisfied with their online marketing, but who were actually in a poor market or with a competition that was much more efficient and convenient (prices, catalogs, logistics).
In short, data is also useful for rethinking your business and understanding where it really is worthwhile investing.

2) Data that reveal information about your audience
Firstly, here is a statistic that always leaves us surprised: 40% of people who buy products for children do not have children at home.
Then there are two sub-kinds of data that we can and must analyze: generic (demographic) and specific (that is, typical of its customers).

Generic data, are simple enough to find (research volumes, statistics, trends, etc.), the specific ones are clearly more valuable and require more effort.

To be clear, if your business was in the theme of children's items, you would find that you can address people who in most cases are buying a gift, but this would be little if you do not understand what kind of gift they intend to buy, what budget they have, which products in the catalog are competitive on the market. In short, this is the anecdote of GreenPal, which saw a significant increase when each message highlighted the main buying drive.

Another moment of analysis is related not only to expectations but with behavior: when people come into contact with products and services? On which channel? At what time? With what device?

The more information you get, the more smart decisions you make. The more intelligent decisions you make, the more relevant you will be.

The last aspect is the data, the information, must necessarily be multi-channel. Come from the entire purchase path or, even earlier, from the people you think you are intercepting. It's when data is mixed and analyze globally that they can really make smart, profitable decisions.

An interesting case is what emerged from a research U Pi Datametrics that analyzed through a social listening tool the conversations of users on various social networks. In particular, he revealed some models: for example in January the main conversations were focused on being free from debts (a very good idea of the beginning of the year!). Instead, searches on Google continued to be constant on credit cards and mortgages.

Here the value of intent is very clear: people are looking for a solution to be free from debts. Without going into financial matters, the solution could also be a mortgage to consolidate all past debts. What makes the difference is therefore what you communicate after you know what people are really looking for.

Starting from the data allows intelligent decisions to be made and thus obtain better results (less money spent, increase in turnover).
We need to focus on important data and let them inspire strategic actions within the company (new products, different approaches, promotions, etc.)
Create an ideal customer profile (buyer personas).
Set up the right technology on the site for correct user knowledge.
We must not make unrealistic hypotheses. Information is almost always available and just waiting to be evaluated.

TACTICS AND STRATEGY

"Marketing is not the art of finding clever ways to dispose of what you make. Marketing is the art of creating genuine customer value" – Philip Kotler

Tactics and strategy are used today in an incorrect way, often attributing the same meaning, sometimes reducing everything to a temporal question: short and long term respectively; finally, there are those who continually place them in opposition.
Indeed, tactics and strategy are linked and indissoluble concepts, sides of the same coin.

Summarizing:
- the strategy is an action plan to achieve a predetermined purpose;
- tactics are the specific ways in which this purpose will be achieved.

In marketing, therefore, the strategy could be for example: to position itself as a specialist in a specific sector, to be recognized as a leader in a low cost market, to concentrate on a single product or service, etc.

The consequent tactics could then be all that includes online promotions, search, content on social media, etc.

Before this, however, it is necessary to determine objectives and objectives that are measurable and which can continually determine how far we are from the result, how much the tactics are actually working.

In fact, we speak of *Smart* objectives:

S = Specific

M = Measurable

A = Achievable

R = Realistic

T = Time-Based

Considering this strategy cannot therefore be something abstract (as well as in the case of "positioning") but well defined.

"If you can't describe your strategy in twenty minutes, simply and in plain language, you haven't got a plan. "But,", people may say, "I've got a complex strategy. It can't be reduced to a page." That's nonsense. That's not a complex strategy. It's a complex thought about the strategy" – Larry Bossidy

---

An example (almost) correct therefore could be the following.

General objective: increase revenues by 20% by the end of the year. Specific objectives: increase the traffic on our site, improve the conversion of sales pages, build customer loyalty, increase the average value of purchases.

Strategy: to intercept people really interested in our products/services by offering relevant content, products and messages. Know the existing customers to propose personalized messages and encourage new purchases.

Tactics: publish interesting content on your blog to intercept users, promote content sponsored on social media, send a specific newsletter, invest in AdWords, optimize SEO to appear in searches, etc.

It is then clear what could be the biggest mistake of a company: focus on tactics without having precise objectives and without having a shred of strategy.

The other big mistake is to use pre-packaged models; objectives, strategy and tactics not customized on your company and on your market.

CUSTOMIZED STRATEGIES FOR RELEVANT RESULTS

"What business strategy is all about – what distinguishes it from all other kinds of business planning – is, in a word, competitive advantage. Without competitors there would be no need for strategy, for the sole purpose of strategic planning is to enable the company to gain, as efficiently as possible, a sustainable edge over its competitors"
– Kenichi Ohmae

Let's review the first example in a personalized way:

- General objective: increase revenues by 20% by the end of the year.
- Analysis: assessing which products and services are most profitable, for which you have a real competitive advantage, define the reasons why customers buy them and have done so in the past.
- Specific objectives: increase the traffic of people's site who show the same problem need of those who have purchased in the past on our site, improve the conversion of sales pages, retain customers who bought that specific product/service, increase the average value of purchases by matching a related product/service.
- Strategy: Communicating a specific message (concerning, for example, that product/service for which you have a competitive advantage) to the right people, at the right time and in the right way.
- Design: Review the messages of our communication (slogans, landing pages and sales, personalized URLs) and make them relevant to the public identified (as in the example of GreenPal).
- Tactics: publish content, ideas, advices on the specific problem on your blog to intercept users really interested, promote sponsored content on social media that invite the action (it could also be reading a post) people interested in that specific topic, send a specific newsletter, invest in AdWords and optimize the SEO to appear in searches related to the public and about a specific need/problem.

What we have described is the simplified model of Search Marketing Design. As you can see, everything is declined in an even more specific and focused way, based on the analysis of the data and defining a work of "design" aimed at communicating in a personalized and relevant way.

Work that clearly does not end here, because there is another aspect that we must always consider: the need to make a choice. Because even in the digital world, you cannot really communicate everything and get everything, you have to focus on what is most profitable.

99% of online people will not buy your products or services. Instead, concentrate on 1% who will be happy to do so.

In fact, there are two further elements to keep in mind: time and channels. You cannot think of being anywhere and anytime unless you want to hurt or squander a fortune.

It makes no sense to be on Snapchat if the "right" people are not there or they might just get us by mistake. It makes no sense to communicate on Sunday mornings if the public is at the park with their children; or you must already estimate that you will have to communicate on a mobile channel and therefore "draw" a mobile message.

To paraphrase Jay Baer, briefly: be (communicate) where (your) world is going.

The data analysis, the market knowledge and the public, allows us to identify correct objectives, which must be realistic and measurable.

The strategy is a specific, personalized plan and not a model that looks good or that has worked for others.

Tactics are the consequence and application of the strategy to achieve specific goals.

You cannot be anywhere and do everything, unless you do it wrong! Better to be focused. Engage where the (your) people are.

PERFORMANCE

"Don't keep doing what you've always done just because it's easy to do!" – Ian Minnis

Among the causes of the lack of success in the digital world there is a certain affection for old things, traditional methods but also what was thought to be the right thing to do. In this new market, on the other hand, we must plan, but also be quick and agile and always taking the most useful and satisfying path.

The data does not belong only to the preparatory phase but will be ready companions to indicate the road on each stage.

When executing a marketing plan one must always keep in mind that everything can be improved (if measurable).

" The success of a page should be measured by one criteria: does the visitor do what you want them to do?" – Aaron Wall

DATA DRIVEN, ROI ORIENTED, PEOPLE FIRST

On this book I wanted to bring into the picture, in a simplified way, the dynamics that regulate marketing and doing business in the digital world, what is the idea behind Search Marketing Design.

The message that I hope to be able to convey is the need to start from data to maximize profit, communicating with people in a relevant way.

"A data driven strategy is a strategy for acquiring, managing, enriching and using data for marketing" – Ian Thomas

---

Data driven marketing consists of taking time to listen and understand people, to learn to speak with them effectively. Understanding the data is understanding people's expectations. And, even in the digital world, people always come first.

Whoever does marketing, who does business, should always keep it in mind.
Data driven, Roi Oriented, People First.

PART FOUR: REAL COMPANY STORIES

DIGITAL AS AN OPPORTUNITY?

PREMISE

Over the last 20 years of experience in the digital world, I have witnessed not only the evolution of technology, digital channels, user behavior, but also the relationship between business and digital.

One of those relationships that in other fields would be considered "complicated", between love and hate, mistrust and curiosity, an unmissable opportunity and an obligatory step.

The first internet sites, rough and expensive, were an opportunity for companies to have an online presence. They represented status, in a sense, but also trust in a technology that could have been bet on and it would have been beneficial to do so.

Then there were the 2000s and the dot.com bubble. In those years, it seemed, at first, that everything that was digital would be profitable, but later that it was all a bluff.

A rude awakening from a dream too good to be true. It took some time for digital to enter real life, people's everyday gestures. Surely the dizzying development of smartphones has been decisive on this sense, bringing the web into everyone's pockets and allowing to reach in real time, far from desks and desktops, a number of people without equal in the history of humanity.

Only in this way is the perception of the importance of the network rooted in every corporate communication strategy, becoming an essential point.

When digital has become inevitable?
When was it understood that it had an impact (to do or not to do) on the destiny of the companies?

I asked these questions to entrepreneurs and marketing directors who, like me, have experienced the digital debut and are living, successfully, this new age that we could define as more mature.

I thank them already for the precious contribution to this book.

1 / COMBINE MARKETING TO COMMERCIAL DEVELOPMENT

by Maurizio Bramezza
Marketing Communication & Purchasing Manager di Midas, world leader in car service and maintenance services.

In my story there have been several important moments, moments in which the company has understood the inevitability of digital. Speaking instead of Midas, my current company, I think you can find as many moments on which to reflect.

First of all I believe that a company like Midas is oriented by tradition, characteristics, offer, to digital communication, or perhaps it would be better to say "to communication in general". I think in fact that companies that take advantage of the online opportunities channels are also those that have proved more open in the past. The story of Midas is an example: among the very first companies to grow in franchising, we speak of the 70s. Another aspect is internationalization and innovation, Midas is born in Georgia and extends today all over the world.

Our proposal is in fact to evolve an unskilled mechanical workshop or a tire shop in a hyper specialized center. With the advent of digital, therefore, Midas immediately believed it was wise, unavoidable, to take full advantage of this channel.

A channel to be exploited not only in terms of lead generation, we could say sales, but also listening and understanding of the market.

Even today we use a lot of online channels to test marketing and development actions. I think it's the real big innovation: being able to start quickly and be able to adjust the route without feeling constrained, overly committed, as it once was.

Another moment that I consider fundamental is my recent appointment as head of the development of the Italian market.

Appointment that is combined with the responsibility of Marketing. Here, marketing and development, together, as a strong and indissoluble binomial, I think it is the real message to be grasped.

The real challenge of the future lies in this, in being able to keep up with a market that is no longer static but constantly moving; as much for us as a company and other operators, as for our customers.

Recently, for example, I have been asked how one can justify, or accept, the investment necessary to switch from an independent tire or mechanic to a multi-service center, especially during these times of crisis.

I replied that I consider it an inevitable passage. Never as in this period should the choice between growth, evolution and closure be evident. Here, the choice between growth, evolution and closure, also passes from this, from the digital. And perhaps it is correct to say that it is inevitable.

2 / STAY BEHIND THE CHANGE, WITHOUT FORGETTING THE HUMAN ASPECT

by Fabio Chisari
Founder e CEO di Azonzo Travel, Tour Operator specialized in tailor-made trips, luxury travel and sustainable tourism.

Azonzo Travel is born on the network. Our business model is based on direct sales to the customer.
Our web is our window on the world, so the digital element has been a fundamental strategic paradigm, essential since the first day of life of the company, now 14 years ago.
When we opened, in 2004, part of our target audience, travelers over 60, still had some difficulty using the network as a mean of communication. But things have changed very quickly.
Within a few years even those aged over 80s have begun to demonstrate familiarity and confidence with the tools of Internet 1.0 that is surfing the web and sending an e-mail, which is why digital has become an essential market.

However, it is necessary to make a very important distinction.
The big operators that sell standardized holiday packages, example, shelf products, must necessarily push more and more on the digital management of the whole process, from the presentation of the product to its sale, with online payment by credit card or other usable payment systems Network. Their business is based on volumes, given that the marginality on the individual product is always lower. And so it becomes vital for them to remove the human element, the most expensive, from the sales process.

For us "artisans", that we mainly package and sell customized services with high added value, it is essential to have a continuous dialogue with customers. So for an operator like Azonzo Travel, digital remains a vital tool for business, but is always linked to the role of communication and CRM.

The real future challenge for Azonzo Travel will be to monitor two things. How the use of the network evolves through different devices (tablet, smartphone, TV), compared to traditional PC use. And how the social world evolves for a qualified and high-end clientele like ours.

Or to understand if and which social channels can still be interesting communication vehicles for high added value services like ours.

3 / NO ONE CAN HIDE FROM CHANGE

by Gabriele Di Matteo
Anchorman Journalist, Senior Media Analyst at RAI - Radiotelevisione Italiana S.p.A.

The Internet discovery, a world parallel to the real one, I did it with exaggerated excitement in the late 90s, when downloading a Web photo seemed an absolute miracle. This is why the *Apriti Sito!* program was born on Telelombardia. Forerunner di Netcafè that I then conducted for 15 years. The most exciting thing we could put on air was the traffic going on a Seattle bridge where they had installed two cheap webcams.

Then social media arrived. That at first they caught me indifferent, they looked like the college bulletin boards where everything was sticky. I had a BlackBerry that I had bought to imitate the IT managers running around the CES stands in La Vegas. And since I had created the "I'm writing a tweet" column during the live broadcast on the Top Tech digital channel (24 hours non-stop technology) now closed and used as a stable for Milanese football, or Chinese. I was distracted by keeping my head down on the keyboard. The viewers wrote me furious. Today, in the liquid society of AI data for robots and machine learning, the www seems something ancient, the same age as the wars of independence.

It is true that every business is today a digital business: no one, from NASA to sushi at home can stay out of the digital fence. A phenomenon that has also created monsters. I find it difficult to explain to my Bocconi friends that Uber, without producing or owning only one machine, has a market value higher than GM and that the Peking startup DIDI which applies AI and Data to mobility, is valued at $ 56 billion.

The platforms have sucked in value to thousands of both commercial and service businesses with locations on Earth.

For the future I expect increasingly complex scenarios. I was very impressed in the sequel to Blade Runner shot by Denis Villeneuve the absence of smartphones in the hands of the protagonists. The forecast is that they will be integrated into the human body with extreme wearable tech projects. And two films made me very distressed. Ex Machina in which the god-like scientist builds and destroys at his pleasure beautiful women robots of different races. Not to mention "Her", where Joaquin Phoenix falls in love with an Operating System so deeply that he presents her by phone to her daughter as "new girlfriend". And I think that the next generations will be so immersed in the digital world that they will not disregard us anymore. Smart machines will be ultra-fast but incapable of creative innovation.

And a cup of hot porcelain emanating the scent of a good coffee on a table in the Galleria Vittorio Emanuele will disfigure all the billions billed by Starbucks.

4 / DIGITAL BRANDING: BETWEEN PERCEPTION AND REALITY

by Gaetano Grizzanti
Business Identity Advisor / Lecturer / Expert of the Court of Milan in Trademark
Founder and CEO of UNIVISUAL Brand Consulting

Less power to the web, more to the brand. In spite of the appearance, this is an absolutely pro-Internet provocation. The network, from the bottom of its virtuosity, has the real power to humanize the brand, establishing a sincere and non-hypocritical dialogue with the user, communicating through a simple and humble approach, without the fear of going unnoticed.

Forced by now even the most skeptical and the most refractory to fall into the Net, it can be said that the panacea of the total connection has sanctioned the definitive paradigm: we are no longer in the era of reality, but in the one of perception.
Starting from the assumption that - confirmed by research on Functional Magnetic Resonance - this paradigm suggests to us that what is true is not true, but what others believe, of a person as a product. It is shown that 90% of our decisions are irrational and not entirely conscious, and it is in this "mental territory", therefore impalpable, that the brand acts, changing the sense of a thing and giving a new meaning, often different from reality objective but so true as to generate concrete convictions.

Today, brands, due to digital interaction, have to expose themselves more than yesterday, forging more authentic ties with people: but in order to exploit this potential, it is necessary to embrace more consistent narratives that are close to the life experience of individuals.

Certainly, in this scenario, the difficulty for companies to control their communication grows. Social channels, for example, convey contents that are able to prevail over those issued by the companies themselves, often returning distorted by the original.

This is where the brand makes the difference. The brands are "avatars" that, in fact, implement a transposition between the most tangible aspects - such as business, product, marketing - with the intangible ones, where the emotional and individual components support the business strategy.

In reality we are talking about something that becomes intangible as extremely tangible, capable as we said to generate convictions hardly irreversible. Trying to change a person's mind is an arduous undertaking, especially when this idea is supported by many voices, as happens with the spread of the web.

It is not enough to affirm the truth to be believed. The brand not only communicates by issuing statements, or exposing technicalities and content related to the product, but it exists and is revealed through a way of being and thinking, emotionally involving men and women, garnering affinity of views, perhaps disseminated through a post on a social-network or the infamous "storytelling" of a corporate blog.

5 / THE DISRUPTIVE CHALLENGE OF DIGITAL

by David Herzog
CEO of Hoval Italia, a company that has been developing solutions for heating and environmental well-being for over 70 years. Its products, synonymous of excellence, high technology and commitment to sustainability, are present in the Vatican City, Windsor Palace and Burj Khalifa.

My first meeting with digital? It was 1995 I worked in an ISP (Internet Service Provider), and it was then that I understood, or rather I began to think, what could have been the Internet and the potential of digital: global change towards a "connected" world. It was just a first step towards the digital transformation of our business today and tomorrow. Yet it was already clear that we were facing something new and revolutionary. A few years later, in early 2000, while I was working in a company that was involved in the development of "Voip carrier network" on a global scale, I started to really know the "disruptive" effect of the digital world for traditional business, in this case the telecommunications.

I immediately invested in Google and Amazon shares because, in my opinion, they were about to change games with innovative business models. We can say that it really went like this.

Today, however, we live a different age, a phase that we could define as "digital awareness" in which each sector is confronted with the question of how to deal with the issues that are posed by the intensity and digital business models of the respective sector.

I'm lucky to work in Hoval, a company that fully captures the amount of these times and the digital. It is a true paradigm shift in which the object begins to communicate with the human support system to increase overall efficiency in the Smart City for a Smart Habitat: a finally sustainable world.

In this context, as a company (company or community?), we wonder how to reduce energy dependency from other countries, introduce renewable energy production and consumption systems, and apply digitization to increase collaboration between systems that provide additional energy savings. Our main objective is the integration of components to 'improve efficiency' and performance in buildings air conditioning. Therefore, digital becomes the means by which we create and offer even more value for our customers. For example, our "IoT Hoval Digital" platform makes energy management more accurate and simple. With the support of artificial intelligence and algorithms that include weather forecasting, we greatly increase the efficiency of the system.

Through the user-interface of the app we allow the user to organize and manage their energy needs (heating, cold, hot water) in an intuitive way, reducing the complexity of system management, for example controlled ventilation in combination with pumps heat. The innovation is therefore able to monitor the process of the system and intervene immediately if necessary.

I think the process of digital transformation must be a priority for every company. The current market is much more complicated and uncertain than in the past. The companies that are winning are those that focus on the digitization of services and processes, which capture the desire of the consumer to get quick and personalized answers that allow to independently manage his services and simplify his life.

Another aspect is given by the composition of the market. In the early 2000s the word "disruptive" began to make sense, but today it has entered both vocabulary and society.

The average life of an S&P 500 company has risen from 67 years of the last century to 15 today, it is expected that 40% of the current may disappear in the next 10 years. Companies that dominate the market did not even exist 10 or 5 years ago.

In more concrete terms, just look at Amazon that today, in the United States, has activated a sales service and installation of boilers. In Italy, companies in the energy sector already offer integrated services to the final consumer. Google offers the Nest platform to give the possibility to communicate with all the devices at home, including heating management. This means that new competition scenarios are opening up in the market to which nobody is accustomed. This through new sales channels such as e-commerce and with increasingly integrated cloud services.

More than ever, Steve Forbes warns: « If you are not the disruptor of yourselves, it will be someone else ».

Here, the challenge of digital could be this: to question oneself, to listen to the client, to experiment, to completely embrace the digital. That's a challenge!

6 / DIGITAL AS A NEW START

by Alessandra Modenese Kauffmann
Swiss Chamber Director, Swiss Chamber of Commerce in Italy.

At the end of the nineties, our Chamber of Commerce, first among the member associations, decided to activate its first website, in the face of the explosion of the network and its services.

The technological and socio-cultural revolution of the nineties (together with other inventions such as cell phones) deeply influenced means of communication.

From a simple static site or showcase site, we then passed over the years to more interactive versions.

The real change for the Chamber, however, arose from the need to transform itself from an association to support the institutions and the requests of the members and in general of Swiss SMEs, a dynamic and proactive reality, able to adapt to the needs of a rapidly evolving and characterized market from strong competition. To allow this change of course, also aimed at total self-financing, it was necessary to engage in communication, similar to any company, to make known services and activities.

It was precisely for this vital purpose that Swiss Chamber, in addition to developing new services, increased its communication activities such as the La Svizzera Magazine, the thematic conferences, together with the creation of Swiss Corner, the well-known innovative space for communication in Milan. But in this evolutionary process the support of the new multimedia communication techniques, which in fact characterized the global economic development, was of fundamental importance.

Today everything that is done or sold is not visible if it is not present on the network or can be downloaded from a smartphone.

For our Chamber of Commerce in particular, visibility on the internet is of fundamental importance, thanks to a targeted SEO activity, precisely in order to reach the primary target group of SMEs, especially in German-speaking Switzerland.

7 / THE NEW DIGITAL PARADIGM FOR MARKETING

by Anna Ponticiello

Business and Marketing Advisor, former Marketing Director

My professional career is emblematic: the speed and impact of digital on our lives are determinant.

After my studies at the University I have worked in serveral agri-food companies, managing famous brands such as Cirio and Del Monte, in a context in which nature and its cycles still had an important weight. It was common that from spring onwards, the company began to monitor the climate, to inquire about frosts and blooms. We became aware of this aspects only from the digital bubble newspapers of the early 90s. Times were not ripe and the context of Food & Beverage was extremely far from the web.

As a marketer I began to explore the potentials of the web only since 2002, using it essentially as an additional channel of communication with consumers: I sensed the possibilties of interactions and I wanted to understand how to take advatage of them. In some cases, perhaps it was too early, for example, in 2003 I remember a fruit nectars promotion for children aged 4 to 10, where we replaced the physical prize with a digital prize for all: a code for access to an online game inspired by fruit. The game was really nice but accesses were very few. On the other hand, other digital projects on food suffered the same fate as, to name one, the Esperya ecommerce, while today we are witnessing the flourishing of many similar initiatives.

In 2006, I decided to leave the Food & Beverage sector into the e-publishing division, which I followed the online services and software for professionals and companies, the company was Wolters Kluwer Italia.

A "technology driven" industry with their BtoB marketing logic, which soon to be invested by the digital transformation.

Even though I had no more daily tastings of new recipes (food has always remained my personal passion), I have dedicated myself to the understanding of a more cultured target and a much more complex and evolving offer.

I believe that the great sensitivity and attention to the consumer was the star comet that guided me in the new path and transposed the responsibility in the elaboration of recipes into the customer experience.

The seek for customer needs has been enriched with new digital channels. The customer focus applied to briefs for large TV campaigns has moved to the design of digital experiences for sites and social media. From the contents of labels to the user information.

As a "tomato expert " I became once again responsible for innovation projects and inside the restricted strategy team for the Digital Transformation of publishing offers: the transition from paper books to ebooks and digital libraries, the evolution from professional magazines to online services and the chunck content sale in pay per view.

It was an experience that has deeply changed me, I did not have the skills or knowledge to work on that area so I searched and studied the information by myself, such as attending conferences or Observatories at the Polytechnico or also web research.

Very often this information was not yet solid, for example when we launched the ebook; the format was not still clear, there was not an established standard so far.

So today, among my passions, further to food, there is the digital innovation.

I want to continue to learn and update my skills on this wonderful digital world. In return, for client - founders I offer methods to listen to their targets and understand the personalities that compose them because - as I often say to my clients - only the happiness-based business takes off.

I do not understand all the acronyms used by real nerds but I have realised that working together we can get fantastic results.

To get out from tradional has meant abandoning certainties and consolidated skills in favor of curiosity and continuous research and transformation. When browsing the digital world I signed up for Badoo thinking it was a social media and the other night I think I showed off by accident on TikTok ...

We are now all aware of the limits of digital and its risks (for privacy, for relationships ..) but I must say that I still perceive its enormous potential above all.

ACKNOWLEDGEMENTS

I had heard that writing a book is one of those experiences you do not understand until you've tried. Now I know it's true.

My thanks go therefore to those who have been my traveling companions, or who have made it all start.

To Jimena my life partner, to Guido precious companion of a thousand chats and who insisted for this book to be born, to Alberto for his practical advice. To Valentino, who has always supported me. To Andrea, brother, friend and mentor. To Davide and Roberta who helped me in writing this book.

And of course to Anna, Angelo, Laura, Valentina, to the people of Cdweb, and to our customers, with whom I've been living this digital adventure for over 15 years.

www.ingramcontent.com/pod-product-compliance
Lightning Source LLC
Chambersburg PA
CBHW021833170526
45157CB00007B/2789